RUDYARD KIPLING: THE BOOKS I LEAVE BEHIND

RUDYARD KIPLING: THE BOOKS I LEAVE BEHIND

BY DAVID ALAN RICHARDS

WITH AN ESSAY BY THOMAS PINNEY

Beinecke Rare Book and Manuscript Library

NEW HAVEN

Yale University Press

NEW HAVEN AND LONDON

EDITING
Timothy Young

DESIGN
HvADesign
Henk van Assen, Amanda Bowers

PRINTING
Thames Printing Company, Inc.

BINDING
Acme Bookbinding Company

LIBRARY OF CONGRESS CATALOGING-IN-PUBLICATION DATA

Richards, David Alan.
 Rudyard Kipling : the books I leave behind / by David Alan Richards ; with an essay by
 Thomas Pinney.

  p. cm.

 "An exhibition at the Beinecke Rare Book and Manuscript Library, June 1–
 September 15, 2007."

 ISBN 978-0-300-12674-7 (alk. paper)
 1. Kipling, Rudyard, 1865–1936—Bibliography—Exhibitions. 2. Beinecke Rare Book
 and Manuscript Library—Exhibitions. I. Beinecke Rare Book and Manuscript Library.
 II. Title.

 Z8465.R53 2007
 [PR4856]
 828'.809—DC22

                                                    2007011957

FRONT ENDPAPERS
"Frontispiece [Kipling With Puppets]", from *A Series of Thirty Etchings By William Strang Illustrating Subjects from the Writings of Rudyard Kipling* (London, Macmillan, 1901.)

PAGE 6
The Absent-Minded Beggar. [The Daily Mail Color Illustrated Edition] (London: 1899).
Damask cotton mat.

PAGE 10
Rudyard Kipling by William Nicholson, from *Twelve Portraits* (first series) (William Heinemann, London, September 1899).

PAGE 12
Detail from advertising poster for *The Jungle Book*. (The Century Co., New York: 1894).

PAGE 17
Detail from: *Kipling's Japan: Collected Writings*. [First Japanese Edition] (Kono, 2000).

PAGE 18
Detail from: *The Jungle Book*. [First (English) Edition] (Macmillan and Co., London, 1894).

PAGE 21
"Frontispiece [Kipling With Puppets]", from *A Series of Thirty Etchings By William Strang Illustrating Subjects from the Writings of Rudyard Kipling* (London, Macmillan, 1901.)

BACK ENDPAPERS
Cabinet card portrait of Kipling by Elliot & Fry, London (1889).

COLORS IN KIPLING

David Alan Richards

To the uninitiated, to the person who has never been bitten by the collecting bug—
I quote Rudyard Kipling himself who wrote, "But who can show a blind man color?"[1]
This exhibition is my attempt to show you color.

Every collection begins with a desire, as well as with some physical object. After a dozen
years of collecting Kipling, I cannot recollect the particular book which was my first
acquisition. The origin of my desire, however, was to better understand two subjects I
first encountered academically while a Keasbey Fellow at Cambridge University, following
graduation from Yale College in 1967 with an American Studies major.

These two subjects were the administration of the modern British Empire, and the cata-
clysm of World War I, which accelerated the emergence of the United States as that older
empire's successor. Rudyard Kipling's life and work seemed a bright red thread running
through both these linked histories. Born to expatriates in India in 1865, he returned to
England for his prep school education, became a journalist in what is now Pakistan, and
married an American in London. After being awarded the Nobel Prize for Literature in
1907, in part for work examining the lives of soldiers who defended the empire's borders
and civil servants who bore "the white man's burden," he lost his only son on the Western
Front in 1915, and died in 1936 fearing that "the Hun" would come again bearing arms.

1 "Home," *Civil and Military Gazette,* 25 December 1891, reprinted in *Writings on Writing,* ed. Sandra Kemp and Lisa Lewis (Cambridge: Cambridge University Press, 1996), p. 38.

2 "Rationale of Collecting," in *Studies in Bibliography,* ed. David L. Vander Meulen, 51 (Charlottesville : University Press of Virginia, 1998), p. 9.

But let me not be too grave. Collecting, of course, is not history:
history is work, while collecting is play. As cogently described by
G. Thomas Tanselle:

The [collecting] process can be analyzed into several components, which
include creation of order, fascination with chance, curiosity about the past, and
desire for understanding.... [T]he gathering of tangible things entails a constant
engagement with contingency, and one is dazzled by the diverse succession
of things that pass one's way....[But w]hat one finds is still a matter of chance.
The connection between collecting and gambling has often been made: both
involve jousting with fate....[2]

The Kipling collector often feels he's jousting not only with fate, but with the man himself. There are so many editions, so many titles, and yet, so few copies of several of them—all results he intended. Kipling's bibliography may be the most complex of any modern writer in English, and the causes are many. His publishing career, including posthumous first editions, extended over sixty-three years (from 1881 through 1944, eight years after his death), and over four thousand separate printings of his work exist. Much of his prose and verse appeared in newspapers and magazines far from the world's literary capitals, and their first book publications were spread over six continents, in India, England, the United States and Canada, Australia and New Zealand, Chile, and South Africa. The author himself sometimes suppressed works after they had been published without his sanction; alternatively, he maintained the practice of including some previously uncollected or unpublished poem or story in all single-volume or multivolume editions (making each a "first edition"). With no international copyright law in the United States until 1891, some American "pirated" editions are true firsts of Kipling's books. Furthermore, many of his single stories and poems initially appeared in limited number copyright editions, while others were also separately printed by private presses, usually without permission; none were offered for sale to the general public.

In consequence, a comprehensive Kipling collection in any single institutional library is rare, even now, despite Kipling's contemporaneity and popularity. My collection, added to the prior donations to Yale by Chauncey Depew and Matilda Tyler (with some examples on display here), makes Yale's among the largest holdings of Rudyard Kipling's books, manuscripts, letters, and ephemera in the United States, rivaling and in some respects surpassing those of the University of Texas, Harvard, and the Library of Congress.

As Tanselle has noted, the "creation of order" must be a collector's first principle. A book collector is merely an accumulator, until order is imposed, and he learns what he has and what he still lacks. For that task, an author bibliography is essential. Kipling has been the subject of four major bibliographies (by Martindell [1922/1923], Livingston [1927/1938], Ballard [1935], and Stewart-Yeats [1959]). Being the type of collector known as a "completist," I set out in 1994 to acquire every book identified in these bibliographies as a Kipling first edition, but did not succeed, because of the extreme rarity of several of his suppressed and copyright editions. Therefore, to somehow possess virtually those titles which I will never actually own, I have written my own bibliography of Kipling, to be published next year. In the twinned processes of collection and research, I have found six previously undiscovered first editions, of which Yale now has the only known copies.

These unique survivors (all pamphlets or leaflets, only one authorized for publication by Kipling) exemplify the "fascination with chance" which infuses the game of collecting. One is a San Francisco concert program for Queen Victoria's birthday on 24 May 1900, containing the first American edition of "Kipling's Auld Lang Syne," written for a Boer War benefit concert held only five weeks before at Bloemfontein, in Africa's Orange Free State. The second is the Canadian edition of his speech at Winnipeg on 2 October 1907, worked up by the local engraver. Another is an unauthorized edition of Kipling's poem "The Explorer," printed in 1911 in 25 copies by Carl Rollins, later printer to the Yale University Press. The fourth, the first book edition of Kipling's great war poem of September 1914, "For All We Have and Are," is entitled The Two Kinds of Courage, published as a Christmas keepsake that year by Eleanor Roosevelt's aunt and uncle (this copy belonged to Eleanor and Franklin). The fifth, Every Ounce In Us, is a St. Louis hardware company's propaganda printing (purchased on eBay) of Kipling's speech at Folkestone in February 1918. The last, a Thomas Cook & Sons brochure published in 1920 for British tourists to the French and Belgian battlefields, begins with a Kipling preface about maintaining decorum at these hallowed wastelands.

These same examples also show how collecting helps satisfy "curiosity about the past." What does the San Francisco concert program tell us about Kipling's literary fame 10,000 miles from the front in the Boer War? What does the Roosevelt Christmas keepsake, titled from a London Times editorial bracing the British population for the coming battles in Europe, tell us about a political household in a country not to join those battles for another three years? What does the hardware company pamphlet's publication say about the American attitude on entry into that war, and Kipling's oratorical fame for framing the issues at stake?

The fourth of Tanselle's components of collecting—less elegantly, the itches that are scratched—is the "desire for understanding." A collector cannot love collecting an author's books without wanting to know more about the author's life and times. The personal inscriptions, holograph poems, and owner's bookplates, in "association" or dedication copies of the chosen author's books, can feed that desire. This exhibition contains copies of:

Plain Tales From The Hills (1888), with the bookplate of a trooper of the 17th Lancers, stationed in Bombay;

Soldiers Three (1888), presented by Kipling to Flo Garrard, his first love and former fiancée;

The Story of the Gadsbys, In Black and White, and *Under the Deodars* (1888–1889), three of a set of six Indian Railway Library titles with sequential presentation inscriptions by Kipling to his married American friend Edmonia Hill, showing the arc of his affection for her;

Kipling's copy of a book on roses from the library at Naulakha, his abandoned home in Vermont, annotated on the flyleaf with a penciled list of nine roses named after famous Britons;

the only bound set of issues of *The Friend* (March–April 1900), the Boer War newspaper controlled by the British Army, marked thirteen times with Kipling's signatures to indicate authorship of his anonymous contributions;

a presentation copy of *Puck of Pook's Hill* (1906) with Kipling's ink-smudged, authenticated fingerprint, and his unpublished, bitter poem "The Coin Speaks," warning of the British Empire's decline through the metaphor of a lost Roman coin;

and, containing Kipling's poem, "The English Way," and signed by Kipling and eighty-four other notable British authors, artists, and politicians, the Duke of Windsor's own (the dedication) copy of *The Legion Book* (1929), a fund-raiser for the British Legion, of which the Duke was patron while Prince of Wales.

The first and variant editions, manuscripts and letters, magazines, newspapers, and sheet music gathered here were assembled in the old ways, through bookseller's catalogues and public auctions in the United States and Great Britain, and by new methods, via internet bookshops and eBay. Without these modern resources, and access to on-line university rare book catalogues—all search and research tools unavailable to past collectors and bibliographers—the scope and size of this collection could never have been achieved. I express my deepest thanks to all the librarians, bookdealers, and fellow collectors who have helped me over the years with this endeavor, and to Yale for giving a permanent home to this celebration of the books Rudyard Kipling left behind.

William Nicholson.

Rudyard Kipling.

A New Book
BY RUDYARD KIPLING

THE JUNGLE BOOK

Published by THE CENTURY Co.

ON COLLECTING KIPLING

Thomas Pinney, Ph.D. Yale, 1960

I. WHY COLLECT KIPLING?

The obvious answer is displayed all around you in this splendid exhibit of his work, the most comprehensive since the Grolier Club exhibit in 1929, seventy-eight years ago. Yet, there is this big difference between that exhibit and this one: the Grolier display was drawn from the collections of many members of the Club, and from those of their friends; the Yale exhibit is primarily the creation of an extraordinary single collector, David Alan Richards.

Collecting Kipling—*really* collecting Kipling—comprehensively, with full knowledge, unsparing thoroughness, and unflagging enterprise, is a daunting challenge.

Here are some of the reasons. Kipling had precocious beginnings; he was not yet seventeen when he went to work as a journalist in India. He had a long and productive career, more than fifty years of steady and abundant production. Kipling never suffered writer's block, never took a holiday from writing, and never struggled to find a subject for his pen. The result is a body of work that has yet to be precisely measured. The matter is complicated by the fact that much of what he wrote, especially in the seven years that he spent writing for newspapers in India, was anonymous or pseudonymous, as was usual in those days. Moreover, much of that early work was contributed to journals that have long since ceased publication and whose issues survive in only one or two places in the world, if at all. The would-be collector of early Kipling is thus condemned to struggle against a near-hopeless scarcity and a serious lack of information.

Not only did Kipling write a lot, he also wrote in a great variety of forms and in every sort of mode, from the farcical to the tragic. Short stories, of course—everyone knows something of those—but few, I suspect, have a full appreciation of their range and variety when taken together. American readers, especially, rarely get beyond the early Indian stories and so miss the rich and suggestive art of such later stories as those collected in *Debits and Credits* (1926) or *Limits and Renewals* (1932). But Kipling is not to be limited to short stories:

he is, rather, the complete Man of Letters. He wrote long fictions, of which *Kim* stands at the head; he wrote plays, travel sketches, essays, just-so stories (he illustrated these as well), jungle books, speeches, inscriptions, and a bewildering number of poems in nearly every meter and stanza form known to English poetry. He was, among other things, a master parodist, who could imitate with perfect fidelity the voices of all the English and American poets, major and minor, and he left a mass of juvenilia.

The collector of Kipling must cope not only with the abundance and variety of Kipling's production but with the fact of his world-wide popularity. He was in his day the most-read and the best-selling of writers in English, and it follows that his work was published in a vast number of separate editions—Indian, English, American, and colonial—to say nothing of the innumerable translations made into dozens and scores of the world's languages, a business that has continued without much interruption down to the present day. The French have just recently added Kipling to the pantheon of the *Bibliothèque de la Pléiade*. Few poets had so many opportunities to revise and polish their work as Kipling did, thanks to the steady stream of new editions and collections that flowed from the press in his lifetime, from *Departmental Ditties* in 1886 down to the final (and far from complete) version of *Inclusive Verse* in 1933. Kipling's own collection of his works, presented by his widow to the British Library, runs to more than 700 volumes of various editions, and that is only a selection.

No edition of Kipling, whether of prose or verse, comes remotely close to completeness, though Kipling has been abundantly honored by this sort of attention. The first collected edition, the Outward Bound, began publication when Kipling was only 32 years old but already had produced enough to justify such an enterprise. Towards the end of his career he was distinguished by his publisher, Macmillan, with a magnificent collected edition printed in elegant typographical design on handmade paper and bound in Nigerian goat-skin. This Sussex Edition, limited to 550 copies, did not sell well when it was published toward the end of the 1930s, while the world was still recovering from the Great Depression. A large part of the edition still lay in unbound sheets in a London warehouse at the time of the Blitz and went up in flames when the warehouse was struck by a bomb. The edition, thus made even rarer, is now eagerly sought by collectors, who have driven the auction price up to around £25,000. The imposing thirty-five large quarto volumes of the Sussex Edition certainly provide a feast of Kipling, but the true collector, looking at them with an informed eye, will think of the many, many items that they do not contain.

Yet another challenge to the collector is presented by the fact that Kipling lived and worked at a time when the commerce of literature was emerging into its fully modern condition—that is to say, it was creating and providing for a mass market. Publishers now operated on an international scale and had to deal with magazine editors, literary agents, syndication, and subsidiary rights. A hugely successful author, such as Kipling, could be and was distributed around the world in many different guises. Kipling complicated matters because of his distrust of publishers, which led him to share out his work among rivals: Macmillan published his prose in England; Doubleday in America; but the poems went to Methuen and the collected poems to Hodder and Stoughton. At various other times he published through Scribners, Heinemann, the Century Company, and Appleton, to name no more.

Kipling was born in the age of steam and of home entertainment, but before his death the movies and the radio had fully emerged; television lay just over the horizon. These new forms of amusement were keen to adapt Kipling. As early as 1910, a film version of his poem "The Vampire" was shot, and in the years down to his death another sixteen films, long and short, were made from his work. The 1930s saw a surge of movie-making drawn from his stories and poems ("Gunga Din," "Wee Willie Winkie," "Captains Courageous," "The Light that Failed") and the Hollywood promotional machine generated much that the collector desires: posters, special editions, stills, advertising giveaways. Walt Disney, of course, translated Kipling into animated cartoons, and that is another region for the collector. Radio plays, stage adaptations ("The Man Who Was" had a long and lucrative run), and musical settings ("On the Road to Mandalay" being only the most notorious) are other forms of adaptation, which dwindle down through calendars, paintings and drawings of scenes or characters from the stories, cigarette cards, decorated cups and plates, and other nameless forms of ephemera. All are collectible.

II. IS KIPLING WORTH IT?

That is no doubt a question to be argued, but I take the view plainly put by C.S. Lewis: "I have never at any time been able to understand how a man of taste could doubt that Kipling is a very great artist." So he is. He has all the qualifications, as they were once listed by T.S. Eliot: copiousness, variety, competence. The copiousness and variety have already been touched on. As to the competence, all one has to do, as Lewis says, is to read him in order to see that. He is a master of language; he possesses great originality; he develops steadily in the practice of his art (the distance traveled between the early and late stories is immense). He is at home in both poetry and prose, a rare achievement. His poetry, though always popular, has not been very closely studied nor very intelligibly presented (the so-called "Definitive Edition," the standard collection, presents a baffling arrangement). Yet it holds many pleasant surprises for those who are prepared to read it without regard to some of the labels that have grown attached to Kipling's name—"imperialist," "racist," "jingoist," and the like.

The ways that Kipling is represented by some critics over the last century is not surprising; their readings may be too superficial or even ignorant of his deeper context. It is true that Kipling the private person as distinct from Kipling the artist is open to unpleasant charges about his prejudices. He didn't like the Indian Congress, or Irish nationalists, or Boers, or Americans, or Germans, and so on, yet these observations pale in the light of Kipling the artist, whose work is founded on deep sympathy with human striving in a world of death and an equally deep admiration for the heroism that carries on the struggle. "Praise Allah for the diversity of his creatures" was one of Kipling's favorite texts, and should certainly not be read, after all, as a motto of bigotry or self-delusion. The truth of this observation is to be found in any candid reading of his work.

By way of conclusion, let me offer a caveat. Kipling's work touches so many areas of human experience—and of animal and inanimate experience as well (no one else has ever given a voice to so many different creatures as he has)—and presents those experiences in so many different lights that it is futile to try to reduce him to a single meaning, or even to a consistent set of meanings. One can find evidence in his work for almost any meaning. One can just as readily find evidence for its opposite. A recent critic, despairing of pinning him down, concluded to call him "Protean." Fair enough; but this does not mean incoherent, or without identity. Rather, Kipling, like all classic artists, while remaining himself, will continue to mirror the interests and values of changing audiences through time.

The great Grolier exhibit, which was in place only for a brief five weeks in 1929, was broken up and its items returned to their different owners; in the course of time most of them have been dispersed. The Richards Collection, the primary and sufficient source of this exhibit at the Beinecke (along with select items from the Depew and Tyler collections), will remain intact and go in its entirety to Yale. Lucky Yale!

キプリングの日本発見

ラドヤード・キプリング
H・コータッツィ／G・ウェッブ編
加納孝代訳

THE BOOKS I LEAVE BEHIND

Rudyard Kipling

The Appeal

If I have given you delight
By aught that I have done,
Let me lie quiet in that night
Which shall be yours anon:

And for that little, little span
The dead are borne in mind
Seek not to question other than
The books I leave behind.

—(PUBLISHED POSTHUMOUSLY, 1939)

For the last decade of the nineteenth century and at least the first two decades of the twentieth, Rudyard Kipling (1865–1936) was one of the most popular writers in the English language, in both prose and verse. He was among the last British poets to command a mass audience, appealing to readers of all social classes and ages. Although his few novels, except *Kim*, were only a mixed success, in the medium of the short story Kipling extended the range of English fiction in both subject matter and technique, and did perhaps more than any other author in the English language to blur the division between popular and high art. This exhibition tracks the development of his work, from journalistic beginnings in India, through sudden and sustained success in England and the United States, and follows his transformation from the exuberant bard and binder of Empire, to the public poet of the battles and cemeteries of the Great War which claimed his only son, to the dismayed observer of the post-war years who resisted the drive for the independence of India and foretold the growing threat of Hitler.

Special attention in this exhibition is given to the bibliographic intricacies of Kipling's printed output. His popularity meant that many editions of his work were issued—with revised texts, variant bindings, in special formats, and especially as unauthorized or "pirate" versions. The books and manuscripts shown here, gathered over the years by keen and discerning collectors, provide a picture of how Kipling's stories and images traveled around the world in an amazing range of formats.

The majority of items on display are from the Kipling Collection created by David Alan Richards ('67, '72 Law), and donated to the Beinecke Library. The exhibition has been supplemented by purchases with Beinecke funds, and also draws from the Kipling collections of Chauncey Depew and Matilda Tyler.

FRONTISPIECE

Wm Strang fec.
DS.

481 (380) Kipling with Puppets.   Final St

THE EXHIBITION

The United Services College Chronicle.

No. 5.   JULY 23, 1881.   Price 6d.

Life in the Studies.

Existence in a form-room on the Corridor must always be more or less a struggle for place.

"The simple rule, the good old plan
That they shall take who have the power,
And they shall keep who can" is most generally adhered to; on the strength of it your neighbour usurps your locker, turns your desk out of its nook, and appropriates all your note paper when he gets a chance. To say the least of it this is annoying, but everything comes to an end sooner or later, and after a couple of years probation there comes a 'Study' with all the concomitant delights of brewing and privacy. Still, daily life then is not uninterrupted bliss. Cocoa cannot be a joy for ever, Tea and Coffee lose their charm in time, and then you begin to take tours of inspection among your old form room acquaintances, to admire the coolness of their quarters (up to their time every form room was abominably cold) and finally to spend a great part of your spare time in them. The Nomadic instinct is strong in everybody and will sooner or later assert itself.

Perhaps the constraint of study life may have something to do in strengthening this discontent. We are bound by laws stern as those of the Medes and Persians—"You are supposed to do this" and "you needn't do that" regulate our entire conduct.

Let us take an instance:

A, a particular friend of yours, comes to your room for a convivial brew. Everything goes off beautifully. The Kettle does not upset, the spoons have not been dropped down the sink by enterprising fags, and A is brimming over with good stories. Conversation is gradually becoming animated on the subject of B.'s defects, when a knock is heard at the door: B. shambles in and asks for the loan of some Algebra questions. Now one of the most binding of our unwritten laws is to invite a fellow to brew at once, if he enters one's study at the time when anything of that sort is going on.

No matter if he object to you, or you to him—You invite B. therefore with a ghastly smile, in words like these. "Just in time, old man, there isn't much left, but I daresay we'll have a cup ready in a few minutes, *Please* stay a bit." (B. is a wet blanket, destitute of tact, A.'s personal enemy and an enormous eater.) He accepts in a hungry manner, which goes

INDIAN BIRTH, ENGLISH SCHOOLING

(1865–1882)

*Of all the things in the world there is nothing, always excepting a good mother,
so worthy of honor as a good school.*
—"AN ENGLISH SCHOOL"

ITEMS ON EXHIBIT

*United Services College
Chronicle,* No. V, July 23,
1881: "Life in the Studies."
[Ill. p. 24]

USCC Prefect List
(Jan.–April 1881).
[Ill. p. 26–27]

Stalky & Co. [First (English)
Edition] (London: 1899)

Photograph of Kipling
at United Services College
(ca. 1881)

Kipling's parents, John Lockwood Kipling and Alice Macdonald,
having married in London on 18 March 1865, set sail on 12 April for
India, where Lockwood was to be Professor of Architectural Sculpture
in Bombay. There, on 30 December 1865, their son Rudyard was born,
named after the Staffordshire lake where his parents had met. Following the custom of Anglo-Indian families, his parents, remaining in
India, sent their children (sister Alice—'Trix'—was born in 1868) to
lodge in Southsea, Hampshire, for five years. In January 1878, twelve-
year-old Rudyard entered United Services College in Westward Ho!,
Devon, where most of the pupils were Army officers' sons. Here he met
George Beresford and L.C. Dunsterville, making up the trio later immor-
talized as Stalky, M'Turk and Beetle (Kipling), the "dusky crew" of *Stalky
& Co.* (1899). In June 1881, headmaster Cormell Price revived the defunct
school newspaper, the *United Services College Chronicle,* and made Kipling
the editor. His contributions (all anonymous) in the seven issues he edited from June 1881 to July 1882 included editorials, essays, and his first
published poems.

Office List.

UNITED SERVICES' COLLEGE, JAN.-APRIL, 1881.

PREFECTS.

6 — Pearse, ma.
507 — Rimington
261 — Baugh
178 — Bellamy, ma.
179 — Heastey, ma.
256 — Didham, ma.
350 — Powell
118 — Townsend, mi.

UPPER FIFTH.

318 — *Merriman
161 — *Grimston, mi.

LOWER FIFTH.

42 — *Edwardes, ma.
277 — *Dury ✗
98 — *Prendergast, ma.
143 — Trent
254 — Moore
326 — Campbell, ma.
91 — Baylay
208 — Berkeley, ma.
133 — Buchanan
159 — Beresford
110 — Thomson
214 — *Errington, ma.

UPPER FOURTH.

10 — Dunsterville
301 — Greig
264 — Kipling
313 — Palmer
181 — Gordon, ma.
65 — Molesworth
199 — Davies, mi.
83 — Gibsone
369 — Walters
201 — Townsend, iii.
252 — Kelsall ✗
184 — Maclean
138 — Morris, ir.

LOWER FOURTH.

102 — Young
44 — Steward, ma.
109 — Murray
144 — Bray, ma.
117 — Phillips
349 — Mackenzie
190 — Heastey, mi.
300 — Owen
289 — Ardagh ✗
328 — Brake
245 — Gibbons
95 — Cox, ma.
311 — Stephen
251 — Longmore
194 — Jones, ma.
360 — Vaughan
217 — Bellamy, mi.
290 — Thomas
243 — Savile
419 — Griffith, ma.
356 — Armstrong
279 — Capper, ma.
286 — Harrison

UPPER THIRD.

271 — Cubitt
279 — Coode
233 — Grant
157 — Morris, iii.
264 — Collum
327 — Campbell, mi.
414 — Pearse, mi.
313 — Bray, mi.
265 — Herford
319 — Roos, ma.
314 — Hinchliff, mi.
154 — Maude
295 — White
436 — Daniell ✗
251 — Heathcote, ma.

LOWER THIRD.

341 — Wilson
287 — Hopkins ✗
320 — Wallace
336 — Bulkeley-Hughes
280 — Beadon
367 — Condon, ma.
384 — Stewart ✗
274 — Hinchliff, ma.
425 — Grey, ma.
335 — Bedingfeld
305 — Pocklington
266 — Stanley-Scott
120 — Gilbert
409 — Beddoes
201 — Willes, ma.
98 — Keats ✗

336 — Hutchinson
232 — Sherriff, ir.
337 — Lyon-Campbell, ma.
372 — Babington, ma. ✗
357 — North

UPPER SECOND.

182 — Gordon, mi.
345 — Puckle, ma.
331 — Sherriff, ma.
363 — Roos, mi. ✗
320 — Davies, ir.
359 — Henderson
202 — Cunningham, ma.
570 — Homan-Mollictt
437 — Babington, ma. ✗
262 — Grimston, iii.
315 — Hinchliff, iii.

LOWER SECOND.

323 — Marquis
431 — Berney
322 — Fraser, ma.
265 — Pearson
86 — Williams
406 — Howlett
352 — Savage
347 — Harvey, ma.
271 — Rice
323 — Fraser, mi.
338 — Marsh, ma. ✗
321 — Hulseberg
373 — Ritchie
324 — Fraser, iii.
438 — Willes, mi.
431 — Winterscale
429 — Wooldridge, ma.

UPPER FIRST.

426 — Grey, mi.
342 — Wheeler
389 — Price
248 — Wren, ma. ✗
362 — Errington, mi.
423 — Haviland, ma.
346 — Ashby
347 — MacDonald
251 — Dopping-Hepenstal
257 — Didham, mi.
361 — Prendergast, mi.
358 — Gordon, iii.
329 — Cooper
355 — Puckle, mi.
378 — Maclagan
383 — Caylon
310 — Wren, mi.
306 — Jones, mi.
370 — Hewett, ma.
364 — Keyworth ✗
348 — Harvey, mi.
381 — Sparks
385 — Coningham, ma.
430 — Wooldridge, mi.

LOWER FIRST.

366 — Steward, mi.
166 — Bray, iii.
368 — Condon, mi.
377 — Douglas ✗
354 — Loch, ma.
390 — Pennycuick, ma.
397 — Edwardes, mi.
400 — Hody-Cox ✗

Junior School.

420 — Griffith, mi.
386 — Preedy
388 — Burton, ma. ✗
403 — Hanson, ma.
427 — Kilroy
384 — Hinchliff, ir.
399 — Loch, mi.
405 — Lowis
387 — Capper, mi.
407 — Green
392 — Jobling
393 — Lyon-Campbell, mi.
386 — Coningham, mi.
391 — Pennycuick, mi.
389 — Ploomer
394 — Prendergast, iii.
401 — Brown
398 — Marsh, iii. ✗
376 — Travers
411 — Heathcote, mi.
428 — Merrick
433 — Price, iii.

Preparatory School.

410 — Hewett, mi.
412 — Pennycuick, iii.
416 — Lowry
404 — Hanson, mi.
413 — Cox, mi.
424 — Haviland, mi.
417 — Smyly
422 — Dempster
396 — Burton, mi. ✗
408 — Stapleton
414 — Manderson
434 — Lane
432 — Gunter ✗
440 — Hay ✗

* Sub Prefects.
✗ Day Boys.

26

Ment. Wilson

Please print 25 of these books with
numbers for the Office — on better
paper — as soon as possible.

J. E. Bunting
Lt Col
&c.

I also require 50 copies of the first 6 pages
of blue book (unbound) for the office.

JEB

ECHOES

BY TWO WRITERS.

LAHORE: THE "CIVIL AND MILITARY GAZETTE" PRESS.

THE FAMILY SQUARE

(1881–1885)

I could never stand the Plains / Think of blazing June and May,
Think of those September rains / Yearly till the Judgment Day!
—"A BALLADE OF BURIAL"

ITEMS ON EXHIBIT

Schoolboy Lyrics [First (Indian) Edition, first issue] (Lahore: 1881). The Bradley Martin copy.

Schoolboy Lyrics [First (Indian) Edition, second issue] (Lahore: 1881) Presentation copy from Lockwood Kipling to Col. Thornton. Depew Collection.

Echoes by Two Writers. [First (Indian) Edition] (Civil and Military Gazette Press, Lahore: 1884).
[Ill. p. 28]

Quartette, The Christmas Annual of The Civil & Military Gazette, by Four Anglo-Indian Writers [First (Indian) Edition] (Lahore: 1885).

Beast and Man In India. A Popular Sketch of Indian Animals In Their Relation With People. [First (English) Edition] by John Lockwood Kipling. (London: 1891) Lockwood dedicated this book "To the Other Three," and provided seventy-one illustrations besides the main text. Rudyard contributed the title poems "Oonts!" and "At Sunset," and verse headings for nine chapters.

While fifteen-year-old Rudyard was still at school in Devon, England, his parents arranged in 1881 for twenty-three of their son's poems to be "printed for private circulation only" under the title *Schoolboy Lyrics*, in an edition of fifty copies from the press of the *Civil and Military Gazette*, the local newspaper in Lahore, to which the senior Kiplings had moved in 1875. Copies are found in both brown and white covers, the brown seemingly earlier.

In November 1882, Kipling rejoined his family in Lahore in northeast India, beginning work as assistant to the editor of the *CMG*, and was soon reporting and writing for that newspaper and others in the region. In August 1884, when Rudyard was nineteen and his sister Trix sixteen, their parents published the teenagers' *Echoes* in an edition of 150 copies. These thirty-nine poems (thirty-two later claimed by Rudyard in his *Early Verse* [1900]) were "echoes" or parodies of famous Romantic and Victorian poems, composed when the family spent a holiday month together in the hill station of Dalhousie. Priced at 1 rupee, the edition sold out, and the profits enabled Rudyard to buy a horse.

The final production of "the Family Square" was *Quartette*, published on 19 December 1885 in an edition of 250 copies as "The Christmas Annual of The Civil & Military Gazette" (there was never another). Its "Four Anglo-Indian Writers" are nowhere identified in the book.

DEPARTMENTAL DITTIES

(1886–1899)

A scrimmage in a Border Station — | A canter down some dark defile —
Ten thousand pounds of education | Drops to a ten-rupee jezail —
—"ARITHMETIC ON THE FRONTIER"

ITEMS ON EXHIBIT

Departmental Ditties and Other Verses. [First (Indian) Edition] (Lahore: 1886). The Frank Brewer Bemis/ A. S. Rosenbach copy.
[Ill. p. 30]

Departmental Ditties and Other Verses. [Second (Indian) Edition] (Calcutta: 1886).

Departmental Ditties and Other Verses. [Third (Indian) Edition]. (Calcutta: 1888). [yellowish green cloth boards variant and reddish brown cloth variant]

Departmental Ditties and Other Verses. [First English / Fourth Indian Edition] (London and Bombay: 1890). The Edmund Yates/Ellis Ames Ballard copy.

Departmental Ditties and Other Verses. [First (American) Facsimile Edition] (New York: 1899). One of 250 copies.

Photograph of Kipling by Bourne & Shepherd of Simla, Calcutta and Bombay, c. 1888.

Although *Schoolboy Lyrics* and *Echoes* had already been privately published, Kipling always called *Departmental Ditties and Other Verses* his "first book." Printed in June 1886 on the newspaper press of the *Civil and Military Gazette* in 500 copies and advertised both in the paper and by reply postcards sent by the author "from Aden to Singapore, and from Quetta to Colombo," it was made up to resemble an Indian Civil Service District Officer's government envelope, secured with red tape. Kipling's name appears only in autograph facsimile on the front wrapper. The twenty-six poems were printed only on the verso side of the leaves, from types set for the Indian newspapers in which they had first appeared.

The Second Edition, containing five new poems (not previously printed in periodicals), appeared in September 1886, in an edition of 750 copies, published by Kipling's first commercial publisher, Thacker, Spink and Co. of Calcutta, bookseller and publisher to various government departments. With the Third Edition of April 1888, containing ten new poems and probably also in an edition of 750 copies, the publisher upgraded the binding to calico cloth boards in two different colors.

The First English/Fourth Indian Edition was published in February 1890 by Thacker, Spink & Co. in London and Bombay, with a further ten poems, including "The Betrothed" ("A woman is only a woman, but a good cigar is a Smoke').

In 1899, renowned American printer Theodore De Vinne prepared an unauthorized facsimile edition of the 1886 original in 250 copies for New York publishers Mansfield & Wessels, reproducing the Indian first edition except for the CMG seal and imprint.

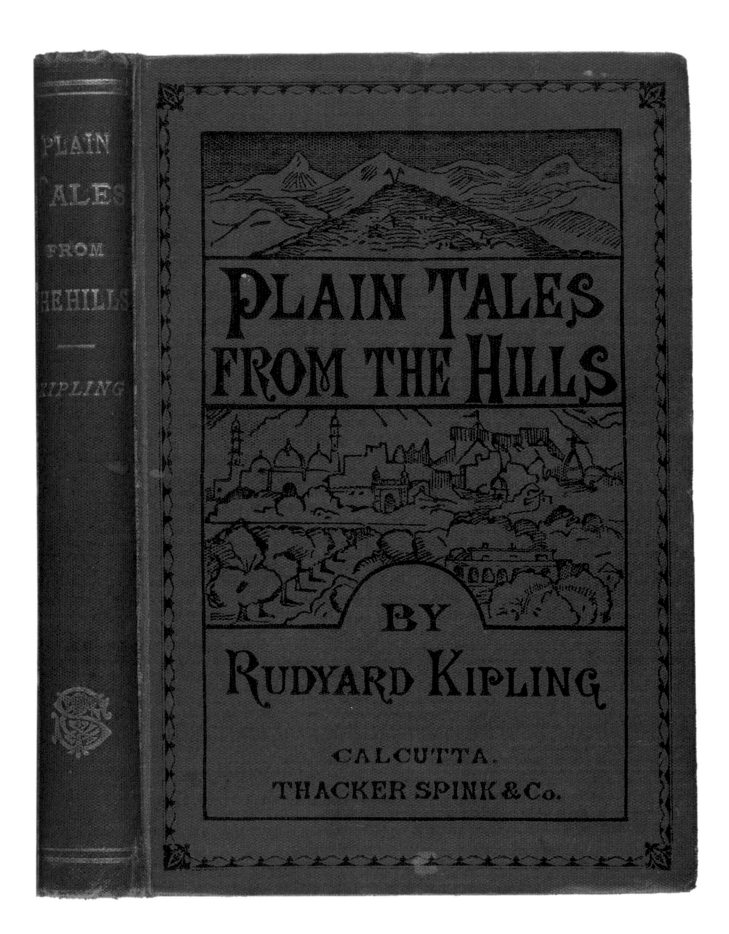

PLAIN TALES FROM THE HILLS
(1888–1889)

I know a case. But that is another story.

—"FALSE DAWN," PLAIN TALES

Thirty-nine short stories appeared in the *Civil and Military Gazette* from
11 November 1886 through 10 June 1887, under the serial title "Plain Tales
from the Hills," without authors' names. Kipling collected twenty-nine
of the stories he had written, together with eleven new stories not in the
original newspaper series, and placed the book with Thacker, Spink &
Co. of Calcutta, which had brought out the Second Edition of *Departmental
Ditties* in 1886. The first issue of *Plain Tales from the Hills* was in a plain
olive green binding, produced in perhaps only nine copies and forwarded
to the impatient author for pre-publication distribution. The cover of the
standard trade edition, published on 5 March 1888 in 1,250 copies bound
in "citron Indian" olive cloth, bears a pictorial design of hills and plains
designed by his father Lockwood. The Second Indian/First English Edition appeared in both Calcutta and London in an edition of 2,500 copies
with a slightly revised text.

A bound volume of Kipling's letters to Thacker, Spink & Co., beginning
in July 1886 and ending in January 1890, regarding the commercial terms
of publication for the various editions of *Departmental Ditties* and *Plain
Tales*, appeared at auction in 1991 and was acquired by Matilda Tyler and
given to Yale. In 2001, Professor Thomas Pinney and David Alan Richards
published a scholarly edition of this correspondence.

Other newspaper stories of Kipling's were published in a series of
quarterly paperbacks from the Civil and Military Gazette Press in twelve
issues appearing quarterly from May 1888 through February 1890; the
first nine contained stories or sketches by Kipling. The title of the series—
"Turn-Overs"—comes from their location in the newspaper, beginning
on the right-most column of page one, and ending in the first column
of page two.

THACKER, SPINK & CO.

Received of

the sum of Five hun

Title & Copyright o

Ditties

R^s 500/-

cutta.   Nov: 18th 1887.

as Thacker Spink & Co

red Rupees, for the sale

he book Entitled 'Departmental

Rudyard Kipling

23

Allahabad.

Nov: 20: 1889.

To Thacker Spink & Co

Gentlemen

As my signed receipt will
have told you I have received
the first half notes for ~~the~~ the
Rs 500 for the D.D.S. and the closing
acct for the sale of the copies.
of the 2nd Edition.

Please send the remaining half
notes to me at Allahabad c/o G. W. Allen
Esq. Pioneer Press.

I go out into the desert tomorrow
and it will be hopeless to find me
there. If you get the Third edition
of the D.D's ready by the 20th
of December I shall on that date
be able to correct them and will
send them back to you at once.
as I shall then be in Allahabad
for fourteen days preparatory to
starting out on another tour
of six weeks or more.

I dare say that your remarks
as to the interest of the publisher
being increased by his interest in
the book he publishes

is quite true. As you will
take 75 per cent of the profits
of the Plain Tales I trust you
will be sufficiently interested.
It seems to me that the D.D.s might
with advantage be put out on
the Railway bookstalls which
now seem to do an extensive
trade in translations of bad
french novels.
I presume that you will undertake
all the arrangements for
getting the Plain Tales reviewed
by the Indian and Home papers.
Kindly send me up half a dozen
copies of the first as soon as the
book is ready for I have some
friends in England who I know
can get it well reviewed for
me. I should like to get the
books by the 20th of December
and I trust that there will
be no defficulty in doing so.
  Yours Sincerely
    Rudyard Kipling

IN BLACK AND WHITE

BY RUDYARD KIPLING.

A.H. WHEELER & Co's.

No.3

ONE RUPEE.

INDIAN RAILWAY LIBRARY

MAYO SCHOOL OF ART, LAHORE,

THE INDIAN RAILWAY LIBRARY

(1888–1891)

I have written the tale of our life | For a sheltered people's mirth,
In jesting guise – but ye are wise | And know what the jest is worth.
—"PRELUDE"

Kipling contributed to several newspapers in India, including the *Week's News* of Allahabad. An Allahabad firm, A. H. Wheeler & Co., had the monopoly on bookstall sales for the Indian railway stations, and its senior partner Emile Moreau conceived the idea of publishing a series of Kipling's stories under the generic title of the Indian Railway Library. *Soldiers Three* was the first number, followed by *The Story of the Gadsbys, In Black and White, Under the Deodars, The Phantom 'Rickshaw,* and *Wee Willie Winkie.* The lithographed covers were designed by the author's father Lockwood Kipling. These little paperbacks created the first Kipling boom: carried by travelers and tourists all over Asia and then the wider world, they won the notice in London and New York that *Departmental Ditties* and *Plain Tales* had yet to achieve. *The City of Dreadful Night and Other Places* appeared in 1891 as No. 14 in the series.

The First English Editions of the Railway Library titles were published in London in 1890 by Wheeler and the London firm of Sampson Low, Marston, Searle & Rivington, Limited. Among the author's known presentation copies of the six Indian editions, one of each went to Mrs. Edmonia Hill, the American wife of a professional meteorologist with whose family Kipling boarded in Allahabad and later traveled by ship to the United States (three of these copies are shown here, two are at the University of Texas at Austin, and one is at present unlocated).

I have eaten your bread & salt,
  I have drunk your water & wine —
The deaths ye died I have watched beside
  And the lives that ye led were mine.

Was there aught that I did not share
  In vigil or toil or ease —
One joy or woe that I did not know
  Dear hearts across the seas?

I have written the tale of our life
  For a sheltered peoples mirth
In jesting guise but ye are wise
  And ye know what the jest is worth.

PUBLISHED AND IN AMERICA
(1890–1891)

Because you steal the property of a man's head, which is more his particular property than his pipe,
his horse, or his wife,…and because you print the stolen property aforesaid very vilely and uncleanly,
you shall be cursed from Alaska to Florida and back again.
—*THE PIONEER,* 9 NOVEMBER 1889

Because the United States did not enact legislation that protected the copyright of British authors in America (and then only as to new material) until passage of the Chase Act in July 1891, everything that Kipling wrote before that date was in the public domain in this country. Thus, they were available for publication in the United States by any commercial printer— referred to as a "pirate" by the authors whose works were "stolen." On his way to London in 1889 after permanently quitting India, Kipling saw an advertisement in a bookshop in Nikko, Japan for a planned edition of *Plain Tales* in New York publisher George Munro's Sons' Seaside Library, and pronounced his "curse on America," quoted above, in the travel letter subsequently published in the Allahabad newspaper *The Pioneer.* (This passage was omitted when these travel letters were reprinted in 1899 in *From Sea to Sea.*)

Upon reaching London, Kipling met Wolcott Balestier, the American agent of New York publisher John W. Lovell. In the absence of copy- right, Lovell recruited British writers by offering a ten percent royalty arrangement for use of advance sheets (or, in Kipling's case, the Indian editions of the Railway Library titles). Thus Lovell (and Kipling) could beat, if not completely forestall, other potential American pirate publish- ers. For *Plain Tales,* Lovell paid the author £10 outright and ten percent thereafter in royalties. Therefore the First American Edition of *Plain Tales* appeared under the Lovell imprint, and "authorized editions" of all the Indian Railway Library titles (the texts sometimes combined) followed in due course. But without copyright restriction, other American publish- ers were free to reprint the pre-1891 Kipling titles, and did so, initiating Kipling's long litigation war in the United States against the "pirates" (in July 1899, according to the *Literary Digest,* he had twenty-three lawsuits in progress against American publishers and booksellers). Lovell's most famous edition of Kipling, *Departmental Ditties, Barrack-Room Ballads and Other Verses,* included poems appearing for the first time anywhere in that edition.

CHAPTER I.

--------++++++++++--------

How Dick and Maisie shot with pistols and how
Amomma eat the cartridges. What happened between Fort
Keeling and the Sea Poppy and how Dick received his soul.

--------++++++++++--------

So we settled it all when the storm was done,
As comfy as comfy could be;
And I was to wait in the barn, my dears,
Because I was only three,
And Teddy would run to the rainbow's foot,
Because he was five and a man;
And that's how it all began, my dears,
And that's how it all began.

Big Barn Stories.

"What do you think she'd do if she caught us? We
oughtn't to have it, you know," said Maisie.

"Beat me and lock you up in your bedroom," Dick
answered, without a moment's hesitation. "Have you got
the cartridges?"

"Yes; they're in my pocket, but they are joggling
horribly. Do pin-fire cartridges go off of their own
accord?"

"Don't know. Take the revolver, if you are afraid,
and let me carry them."

"I'm not afraid." Maisie strode forward swiftly a'

1

LIPPINCOTT'S

MONTHLY MAGAZINE.

JANUARY, 1891.

THE LIGHT THAT FAILED.

CHAPTER I.

So we settled it all when the storm was done,
As comfy as comfy could be;
And I was to wait in the barn, my dears,
Because I was only three,
And Teddy would run to the rainbow's foot,
Because he was five and a man;
And that's how it all began, my dears,
And that's how it all began.

Big Barn Stories.

"WHAT do you think she'd do if she caught us? We oughtn't to have it, you know," said Maisie.

"Beat me, and lock you up in your bedroom," Dick answered, without hesitation. "Have you got the cartridges?"

"Yes: they're in my pocket, but they are joggling horribly. Do pin-fire cartridges go off of their own accord?"

"Don't know. Take the revolver, if you are afraid, and let me carry them."

"I'm not afraid." Maisie strode forward swiftly, a hand in her pocket and her chin in the air. Dick followed with a small pin-fire revolver.

The children had discovered that their lives would be unendurable without pistol-practice. After much forethought and self-denial, Dick had saved seven shillings and sixpence, the price of a badly-constructed Belgian revolver. Maisie could only contribute half a crown to the syndicate for the purchase of a hundred cartridges. "You can save better than I can, Dick," she explained: "I like nice things to eat, and it doesn't matter to you. Besides, boys ought to do these things."

Dick grumbled a little at the arrangement, but went out and made

3

THE LIGHT THAT FAILED
(1890–1939)

Roses red and roses white | Plucked I for my love's delight
She would none of all my posies – | Bade me gather her blue roses.
—"BLUE ROSES," THE LIGHT THAT FAILED

ITEMS ON EXHIBIT

The Light That Failed,
199-leaf typescript,
with 975 changes in
Kipling's hand, and
covering letter to the
Editor of Lippincott's
Magazine (1890)
[Ill. p. 42]

The Light That Failed,
Lippincott's Magazine
(January 1891), Melbourne
(earliest), New York,
and London editions.
[Ill. p. 42]

The Light That Failed.
[First (American) Edition]
(New York: December 5,
1890), twelve chapters,
'happy' ending, inscribed
by Edmond Gosse "pos-
itively the earliest of the
various editions."

The Light That Failed.
[English Pocket Edition]
(London: 1927), presenta-
tion copy from Flo Garrard
to Frances Egerton.

The American journalist J. B. Lippincott sought to promote new authors with something shorter and livelier than the "three-decker" of the Victorian generation; his medium was a monthly magazine, published in New York, London, and Melbourne, with a complete new novelette (50–60,000 words) in every number. The issues of 1890 began with A. Conan Doyle's *The Sign of the Four* (January), continued with Oscar Wilde's *The Picture of Dorian Gray* (July), and concluded with Kipling's *The Light That Failed*, appearing in December, but cover-dated January 1891.

The text in the magazine contains the "happy ending" (hero and heroine engaged to be married on the last page). Sale of the Lovell paperback edition of twelve chapters, although cover-dated December 5, 1890, was held up until *Lippincott's* appeared on the newsstands. Lovell also deposited for copyright a hardcover of fourteen chapters, with the "sad ending" (in which the hero dies in battle). The English first edition, in fifteen chapters with still more text, also had the sad ending. In 1921, Kipling told his American publisher, Frank Doubleday, that he could not then reconstruct the story of the two endings, but it is believed that *Lippincott's* editors urged a shorter, cheerier version for the magazine appearance.

The story was adapted several times, for the stage (1891, New York; 1903, London) and the motion picture screen (1916, 1923, and 1939). These productions inspired illustrated reissues of the novel. The true-life model for "Maisie" was Kipling's first love, Violet ("Flo") Garrard, who in 1927 presented a copy of the book to her companion of her later years, Frances Egerton, denigrating "this singular if somewhat murky story."

The Naulahka

A STORY OF

WEST AND EAST

EARLY LONDON SUCCESS
(1891–1894)

Oh, East is East, and West is West, and never the twain shall meet
Till Earth and Sky stand presently at God's great Judgment Seat.
—"THE BALLAD OF EAST AND WEST"

With the English editions of the Indian Railway Library having made his name in London, Kipling's new work was eagerly sought. *Life's Handicap* (August 1891) was a collection of twenty-seven more Indian stories—including "The Courting of Dinah Shadd" and "Without Benefit of Clergy"—and one poem. *The Naulahka* (June 1892) had begun as Kipling's only serious effort at joint authorship of fiction, with his American friend and Lovell's agent Wolcott Balestier. After Balestier's untimely death on 6 December 1891, Kipling finished writing the novel on his honeymoon, having married Balestier's sister Caroline in a hastily arranged London wedding on 18 January 1892 (Henry James gave away the bride).

Kipling continued to publish in periodicals, sending stories and poems to *The St. James's Gazette, Macmillan's Magazine,* and *The Scots Observer,* renamed *The National Observer,* edited by William E. Henley, who in 1892 included Kipling as the last and youngest English poet to be reprinted in Henley's collection *Lyra Heroica. Many Inventions* (fourteen stories, including "My Lord the Elephant," and two poems) appeared in 1893.

The young author became a celebrity, both photographed as a man about town and caricatured by "Spy" for *Vanity Fair,* and a clubman, selected to dine with the Sette of Odd Volumes, which soon published his witty letter declining the invitation.

consisted of the reproduction of a pencil sketch by the donor, entitled "The Victualling Crew."

The Menu was designed by Mr. Joseph Grego and presented to the Sette by the *Artificer*.

Mr. Rudyard Kipling who had been invited to this meeting but was unable to be present, replied in the following terms :

"To CERTAIN ODD VOLUMES,

"Folios, quartos, and octavos and all others innominate from a small Pamphlet, Salutation :

"For the kindness of that invitation all thanks to your Bound and Beautiful Selves. For myself, Sorrow, since upon that day I am out upon Loan for such hours as you mention.

"Yet, seeing that Odd Volumes do notoriously circulate beyond the use of Complete Sets, it is my hope that I may later meet you, Individual or Collect on the shelves of that great Library

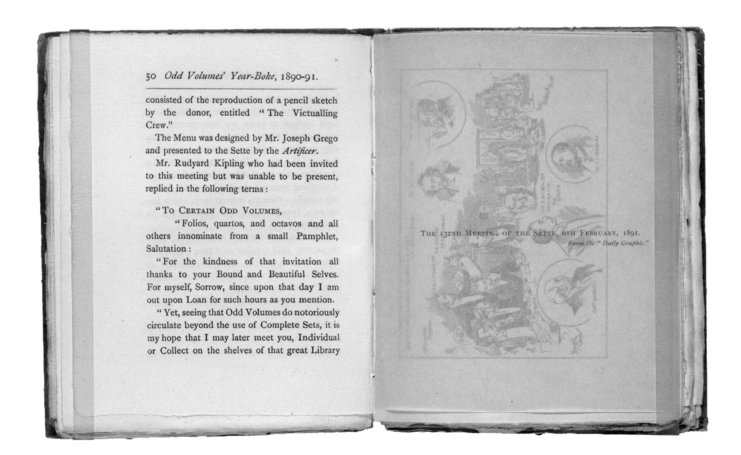

THE 132ND MEETING OF THE SETTE, 6TH FEBRUARY, 1891.
From the "Daily Graphic."

which, lacking all Catalogues, men are content to call the World.

"Rudyard Kipling."

Friday, March 6th, 1891. This was the annual business meeting of the Sette and no guests were present.

The Rules were revised, as usual.

Brothers East, Ball, and Cooke obtained leave to change their titles to *Landscape Painter, Painter Etcher,* and *Mechanick* respectively.

His Oddship presented to the Brethren a specially designed Portfolio in which to preserve the "Folia:" No. 1 of which had been distributed at the previous meeting by the *Ancient Mariner.*

Dr. Garnett of the British Museum presented to the Sette, through the medium of the Secretary, his book, "Twilight of the Gods."

Friday, April 3rd, 1891. The toast of the "Guests" was responded to by Mr. W. T.

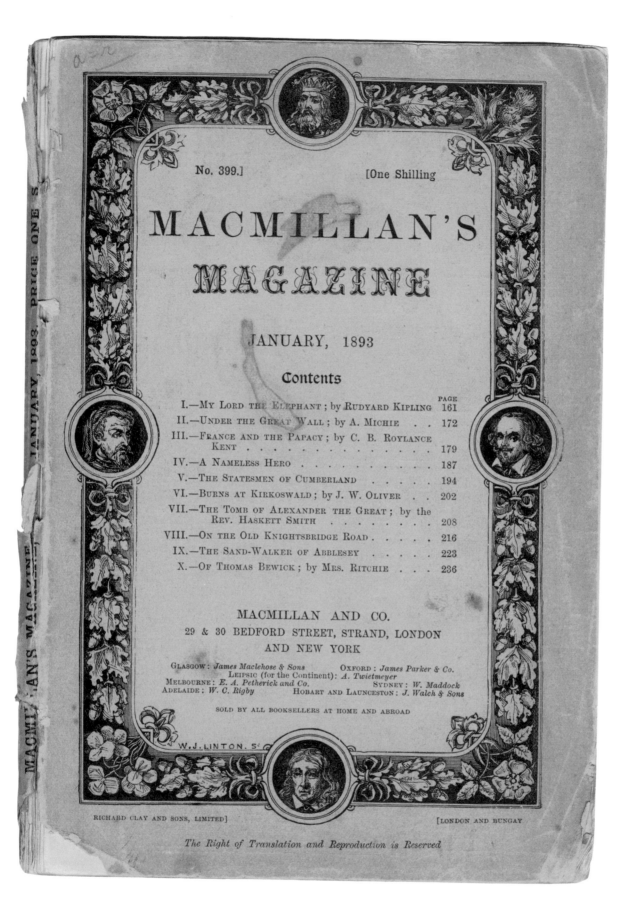

No. 399.]   [One Shilling

MACMILLAN'S MAGAZINE

JANUARY, 1893

Contents

MACMILLAN AND CO.

29 & 30 BEDFORD STREET, STRAND, LONDON
AND NEW YORK

GLASGOW: *James Maclehose & Sons*   OXFORD: *James Parker & Co.*
LEIPSIC (for the Continent): *A. Twietmeyer*
MELBOURNE: *E. A. Petherick and Co.*   SYDNEY: *W. Maddock*
ADELAIDE: *W. C. Rigby*   HOBART AND LAUNCESTON: *J. Walch & Sons*

SOLD BY ALL BOOKSELLERS AT HOME AND ABROAD

W.J. LINTON. Sc

RICHARD CLAY AND SONS, LIMITED]   [LONDON AND BUNGAY

The Right of Translation and Reproduction is Reserved

MACMILLAN'S MAGAZINE.

JANUARY, 1893.

MY LORD THE ELEPHANT.

TOUCHING the truth of this tale there need be no doubt at all, for it was told to me by Mulvaney at the back of the elephant-lines, one warm evening when we were taking the dogs out for exercise. The twelve Government elephants rocked at their pickets outside the big mud-walled stables (one arch, as wide as a bridge-arch, to each restless beast), and the *mahouts* were preparing the evening meal. Now and again some impatient youngster would smell the cooking flour-cakes and squeal; and the naked little children of the elephant-lines would strut down the row shouting and commanding silence, or, reaching up, would slap at the eager trunks. Then the elephants feigned to be deeply interested in pouring dust upon their heads, but, so soon as the children passed, the rocking, fidgeting, and muttering broke out again.

The sunset was dying, and the elephants heaved and swayed dead black against the one sheet of rose-red low down in the dusty grey sky. It was at the beginning of the hot weather, just after the troops had changed into their white clothes, so Mulvaney and Ortheris looked like ghosts walking through the dusk. Learoyd had gone off to another barrack to buy sulphur ointment for his last dog under suspicion of mange, and with delicacy had put his kennel into quarantine at the back of the furnace where they cremate the anthrax cases.

"*You* wouldn't like mange, little woman?" said Ortheris turning my terrier over on her fat white back with his foot. "You're no end bloomin' partic'lar, you are. 'Oo wouldn't take no notice o' me t'other day 'cause she was goin' 'ome all alone in 'er dorg-cart, eh? Settin' on the box-seat like a bloomin' little tart, you was, Vicy. Now you run along an' make them 'uttees 'oller. Sick 'em, Vicy, loo!"

Elephants loathe little dogs. Vixen barked herself down the pickets, and in a minute all the elephants were kicking and squealing and clucking together.

"Oh, you soldier-men," said a mahout angrily, "call off your she-dog. She is frightening our elephant-folk."

"Rummy beggars!" said Ortheris meditatively. "Call 'em people, same as if they was. An' they are too. Not so bloomin' rummy when you come to think of it, neither."

Vixen returned yapping to show that she could do it again if she liked, and established herself between Ortheris's knees, smiling a large smile at his lawful dogs who dared not fly at her.

"See the battery this mornin'?" said Ortheris. He meant the newly-arrived elephant-battery; otherwise he would have said simply "guns." Three elephants harnessed tandem go to each gun, and those who have not

No. 399.—VOL. LXVII.

M

The Recruits' Progress
(a Song of degrees)

1 The 'eathen in 'is blindness bows down to wood an' stone —
'E don't obey no orders 'less the orders are 'is own.
'E keeps 'is weapons awful ˣ an' 'e leaves 'em all about   ˣ filthy (mucky)
an' then comes up the Regiment an' kicks the 'eathen out.

ital ⎰ All along o' dirtiness all along o' mess —
all along o' doin' things rather more or less
all along of 'abby-nay' 'Kul' an' 'hazar O.!'
Mind you keep your rifle an' your kit just So!

2 The young recruit is 'aughty. 'E drafts from Gawd knows where;
They bid 'im tide 'is stockin's an' lay 'is mattress fair;
'E calls 'it bloomin' nonsense? 'E does n't know no more
an' then comes up 'is company an' kicks 'im round the floor.

alf along o' dirtiness &c

3 The young recruit is 'andled — 'E takes it very 'ard —
'E 'angs 'is 'ead an' mutters — 'e sulks about the yard —
'E talks o' cruel tyrants e'll swing for by-an'-by;
An' the others 'ears an' mocks 'im an' the boy goes off to cry.

All along &c

4 The young recruit 'e larstes — 'e 'ears o' suicide.
'E's lost 'is gutter-devil; 'e 'aven't found 'is pride;
But day by day they kicks 'im which 'elps 'im on a bit
Till 'e finds 'isself one mornin' with a clean an' proper kit.

Gettin' out o' dirtiness: Gettin' out o' mess
Gettin' shut o' doin' things rather more or less
Not so much of abby-nay &c
Learns to keep 'is rifle an' 'is kit just So!

5 The young Recruit is 'appy — 'e throws a chest to suit
You see 'im grow moustaches — you 'ears 'im slap 'is boot.
'E learns to 'ear off cussin' with every word 'e slings
an' 'e shows an' 'ealthy brisket when 'e straps for Barf an' Rings.

Gettin' cured o' dirtiness; Gettin' &c
Much too fine for doin' things &c

6 The cruel tyrant Sergeants they watch 'im arf a year —
They watch 'im with 'is room-mates, they watch 'im with 'is beer.
They watch 'im well-be'aved at the Regimental dance
An' the cruel tyrant sergeants send 'is name along for Lance.

7 an' now 'e's art o' nothin' an' arf a private too-get
an' 'is room they 'ap an' keeps 'im to see what they will get.
They cries 'im low an' cunnin' each dirty trick they can
Till 'e learns to keep 'is temper an' 'e learns to know 'is men.

keeps 'is eye on dirtiness; checks 'em all for mess
Puts 'is foot on doin' things rather more or less
aint content with abby-nay &c
Makes 'em keep their rifles an' their kit just So!

8 an' last as Colour-Sergeant 'oo 'as to be obeyed
'E schools 'is men at cricket — 'e schools 'em at parade
They've always clean an' 'andy — they've always set an' smart
an' So 'e talks to officers which 'ave the Corps at 'eart.

9 'E learns to do 'is watchin' without its showin' plain
'E learns to slip a dummy an' set 'em straight again
'E learns to check a rotter that's beginnin' leave to shirk
an' 'e learns to make men like 'im so they'll learn to like their work.

10 an' when it comes to marchin' 'e sees their socks is right
an' when it comes to firin' 'e shows 'em 'ow to sight
'E knows their tricks an' fancies an' just where they will stand
an' 'e knows when they are comin' an' when they're out o' 'and.

BARRACK-ROOM BALLADS AND OTHER VERSES
(1892 / 1896 / 1903)

There are nine and sixty ways of constructing tribal lays,
And every single one of them is right.
—"IN THE NEOLITHIC AGE"

ITEMS ON EXHIBIT

Barrack-Room Ballads and Other Verses [First (English) Edition] (London: May 1892). Trade issue ; hand-made large paper issue; Japan paper issue.

The Seven Seas. [First English Edition] (London: October 1896). Trade issue; hand-made large paper issue; Japan paper issue.

The Five Nations. [First (English) Edition] (London: September 1903). Trade issue; hand-made large paper issue; Japan paper issue.

Autograph Manuscript Signed, "The 'Eathen", originally entitled "The Recruit's Progress," with marginal illustrations by Kipling.
[Ill. p. 50]

Autograph Manuscript Signed, "C. J. Rhodes," written for T. W. Smartt, Rhodes's fellow cabinet minister in Cape Colony, South Africa.
[Ill. p. 52 53]

Autograph Manuscript Signed, "Bobs," first published in *The Pall Mall Gazette,* for December 1893, first collected in the Bombay Edition of *The Five Nations* (London: 1914) after the death of its subject, Lord Roberts.

From *The Light That Failed* (1891) onward, Kipling settled on Macmillan as the United Kingdom and Colonies publisher of his prose work, but for his periodic poetry collections he used Methuen. The first of that Methuen series was *Barrack-Room Ballads and Other Verses* (March 1892), which collected the greater part of the ballads appearing in *The Scots Observer.* With this edition, Kipling began the practice of selling higher-priced, special issues in addition to the 6 shilling trade issue, printed on Dutch hand-made paper (225 copies, priced at 1 guinea [1 pound 1 shilling]), and on Japan paper (20 copies, signed by the publisher, at 2 guineas). *The Seven Seas* (the first hardcover edition of "McAndrew's Hymn," "Hymn Before Action," and "The 'Eathen") was published in October 1896, also on large hand-made paper (150 copies) and on Japan paper (30 copies). *The Five Nations* (the first hardcover edition of "The White Man's Burden," "White Horses," "The Destroyers", and "The Burial" ["C.J. Rhodes"]) was published in September 1903, in trade, large hand-made paper (200 copies), and Japan paper (30 copies) issues.

C. J. Rhodes,
(buried april 10. 1902)

When that great Kings return to clay
  Or Emperors in their pride,
Grief of a day shall fill a day
  Because its creature died:
But we — we reckon not with those
  Whom the mere Fates ordain
This Power that wrought on us and goes
  Back to the Power again.

Dreamer devout, by vision led
  Beyond our guess or reach,
The travail of his spirit bred
  Cities in place of speech:
So huge the all-mastering thought that drove
  So brief the term allowed
Nations not words he linked to prove
  His faith before the crowd.

It is his will that he look forth
Across the lands he won —
The granite of the ancient North —
Great Spaces washed with Sun:
There shall he patient make his seat
(As when the death he dared)
And there await a people's feet
On the paths that he prepared.

There till the vision he foresaw
Splendid and whole arise,
And unimagined empires draw
To council 'neath his skies,
The immense and brooding spirit still
Shall quicken and control —
Living he was the land and dead
His soul shall be her soul!

Rudyard Kipling.

To J. W. S.

W. H. H. Drake
1 . 9 . 1 . 1

Shere Khan
The
Wicked
Tiger.

THE JUNGLE BOOKS
(1894–1895)

Now this is the Law of the Jungle — as old and as true as the sky;
And the Wolf that shall keep it may prosper, but the Wolf that shall break it must die.
—"THE LAW OF THE JUNGLE"

Among the best-loved and best-known of Kipling's works are *The Jungle Book* (1894) and *The Second Jungle Book* (1895). All of the stories in the first volume, written at Kipling's home in Brattleboro, Vermont, had previously appeared in periodicals, but seven poems were new, while eight of the illustrations were by the author's father. It is thought that this was the first of Kipling's books published by Macmillan to have a dustjacket, of glazed tissue paper, presumably to protect the gilt ornamentation of the spine and front cover.

The First American Edition of *The Jungle Book* was published by The Century Company on the same day as the First English Edition, with illustrations by W. H. Drake, and Kipling thought the American binding beat Macmillan's edition "into little pieces...If that green doesn't fade, it's nearly perfect."

The second volume, with eight stories and eight poems (and a paper dustjacket as we know one today), was published in England three days after the First (American) Edition. To *The Second Jungle Book* Kipling's father contributed thirty-seven illustrations. The Century Company's striking advertising posters for these titles are shown on the ground floor with posters for other Kipling works.

THERE WERE DAYS OF LIGHT AIRS, WHEN HARVEY WAS TAUGHT HOW TO STEER THE SCHOONER FROM ONE BERTH TO ANOTHER.

"NAULAKHA", YALE, AND "CAPTAINS COURAGEOUS"
(1896–1897)

But where his goat's hoof cut the crust – beloved, look below –
He's left us (I'll forgive him all) the may-flower 'neath the snow!
—"PAN IN VERMONT"

ITEMS ON EXHIBIT

Rudyard Kiping's personal bookplate, designed by his father, Lockwood Kipling, while on a visit to Brattleboro (1894).

Postcard of "Naulakha."

Photograph of Kipling in the library at Naulakha.

The Book of the Rose by Rev. A. Foster-Melliar (London: 1894). From Kipling's library at Naulakha.

"*Captains Courageous,*" [First (American) Edition] (New York: 1897).

'*Captains Courageous.*' [First English Edition] (London: 1897). The A. Edward Newton copy.
[Ill. p. 56]

Autograph Manuscript Signed, "Attind ye lasses" (also known as "Mulvaney's Regrets") [On loan from Manuscripts and Archives Department of Sterling Memorial Library]

November 1893 letter to a child in Kentucky, with a drawing of Santa Claus visiting Naulakha.

When their bank failed on the newlywed Kiplings' honeymoon in Japan in 1892, they were forced to return to Caroline Kipling's mother's home in Brattleboro, Vermont, where they bought land from Caroline's brother Beatty Balestier. There they built a house, called "Naulakha", near Mount Monadnock, and their daughter Josephine was born, delivered by Dr. James A. Conland. Kipling worked here on the *Jungle Book* stories and poems, and created a home for his growing family.

In the spring of 1896, the undergraduate Kipling Club of Yale College, inspired by Professor William Lyons Phelps, invited the author to attend its first "annual banquet" in New Haven. Kipling sent his regrets on Naulakha stationery to Club President Gouveneur Morris, Jr. in the form of an Irish dialect poem in the voice of Mulvaney of *Soldiers Three*. Morris read it aloud at the Club banquet of 14 May 1896, and then submitted it for publication (without Kipling's authorization) to the *Yale Literary Magazine*. What he later called "my ribald lines to the Yale boys" were never reprinted in a collection by Kipling.

That summer, with the help of Dr. Conland, who introduced him to the fishermen of the Gloucester, Massachusetts fleet, Kipling wrote "*Captains Courageous*", which was serialized in *McClure's Magazine* from November 1896 through May 1897. When the novel was published in the U.S. by The Century Company on 16 September 1897, it was dedicated to Conland. The English edition was published on 17 November 1897, following serialization in London in *Pearson's Magazine*.

During that eventful summer of 1896, Kipling quarreled with his brother-in-law Beatty over the cost of construction of "Naulakha", and Beatty's trial for assault for threatening bodily harm to Kipling was a humiliation for the author, who ultimately determined to return with his family to England; he visited America again only once, in 1899.

God of our fathers, known of old—

Lord of our far-flung battle line—

Beneath whose awful hand we hold

Dominion over palm and pine—

Lord God of Hosts, be with us yet,

Lest we forget—lest we forget!

✤ ✤ ✤ ✤ ✤ ✤ ✤ ✤

"THE VAMPIRE" AND "RECESSIONAL"
(1897–1898)

I gave it to The Times. I say 'gave' because for this kind of work I did not take payment.
—SOMETHING OF MYSELF (1937)

ITEMS ON EXHIBIT

Autograph Letter Signed, Philip Burne-Jones to Lucy Clifford, 18 March 1897, with self-portrait at easel.

The Vampire. [First American Edition] (Gouveneur, New York: St. Valentine's Day, 1898). [Ill. p. 60–61]

The Vampire. [M. F. Mansfield edition, first issue] (New York: March 1898) One of 500 copies.

Recessional: A Victorian Ode. [First American Edition, boards issue] (New York: 1897). One of 150 copies. [Ill. p. 58]

Recessional. [Illuminated Edition] (London: 1914).

"After" A False Start. (Dover, MA: July 1924). Printed by Harvard College librarian George Parker Winship, from the manuscript at Harvard, and then "suppressed."

Kipling's cousin, Philip Burne-Jones, painted a picture for the Summer Exhibition at London's New Gallery, which opened on April 24, 1897. It depicted a pale, beautiful woman sitting over a sleeping or swooning man. Kipling as a jest for his relative wrote a poem on its provocative theme, entitled "The Vampire," which the delighted Burne-Jones included in the Summer Exhibition's Catalogue, although the author had not authorized this. The verses, like the picture, became a sensation, reprinted in many newspapers in 1897, and then separately in many pirate editions, but it was not collected by Kipling for twenty-two years (in *Inclusive Verse*, 1919). When adapted as the 1915 silent film "A Fool There Was," introducing the "It girl" Theda Bara, the word "vamp" became a permanent part of American slang.

Conversely, Kipling's intentions with regard to "Recessional" could not have been more high-minded and public. The poem appeared in *The Times* of London on 17 July 1897, shortly after the celebration of Queen Victoria's Diamond Jubilee; his cover letter to the newspaper read in part: "Enclosed please find my sentiments on things—which I hope are yours. We've been blowing up the Trumpets of the New Moon a little too much for the White Men, and it's about time we sobered down." Like "The Vampire," "Recessional" was reprinted many times without Kipling's authorization (although it was never copyrighted by him). In 1924 there appeared an unauthorized printing, in a limited facsimile edition, of a discarded draft of the poem with a canceled third stanza, under the poem's original title, "After".

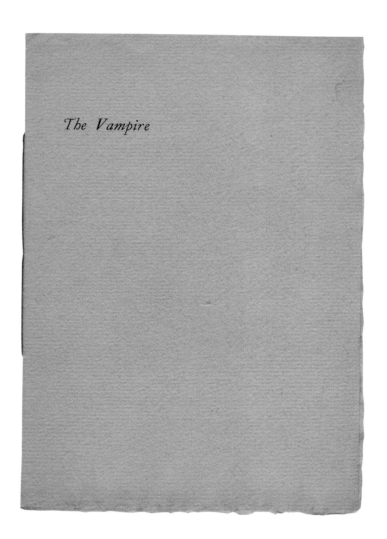

The Vampire

The Vampire

A fool there was and he made his prayer
(Even as you and I!)
To a rag and a bone and a hank of hair
(We called her the woman who did not care)
But the fool he called her his lady fair
(Even as you and I!)

Oh the years we waste and the tears we waste
And the work of our head and hand,
Belong to the woman who did not know
(And now we know that she never could know)
And did not understand.

A fool there was and his goods he spent
(Even as you and I!)
Honour and faith and a sure intent
(And it wasn't the least what the lady meant)
But a fool must follow his natural bent
(Even as you and I!)

Oh the toil we lost and the spoil we lost
And the excellent things we planned,
Belong to the woman who didn't know why
(And now we know that she never knew why)
And did not understand.

The fool was stripped to his foolish hide
(Even as you and I!)
Which she might have seen when she threw him aside
(But it isn't on record the lady tried)
So some of him lived but the most of him died—
(Even as you and I!)

And it isn't the shame and it isn't the blame
That stings like a white hot brand—
It's coming to know that she never knew why
(Seeing at last she could never know why)
And never could understand.

RUDYARD KIPLING.

Written for the picture by Philip Burne-Jones in the New Gallery,
and printed in *The London Daily Mail.*
Reprinted in *The Critic, The Philistine, The Chap-Book* and other
papers.
Now privately reprinted at *The Adirondack Press,* Gouverneur, New-
York, for Laurence C. Woodworth and his friends, Saint Valentine's Day, 1898.

Words written by Rudyard Kipling.

Sung by Miss Fraser at the Press Concert
IN AID OF THE
FREE STATE AND LONDON WIDOWS' AND ORPHANS' FUND.

I.

Be welcome to our hearts to-night, Oh kinsmen from afar,

Brothers in an Empire's fight and comrades of our war.

    For Auld Lang Syne, my lads, and the fights of Auld Lang Syne,

    We drink our cup of fellowship to the fights of Auld Lang Syne.

II.

The Shamrock, Thistle, Leek and Rose, with heath and wattle twine,

And Maple from Canadion snows, for the sake of Auld Lang Syne.

    For Auld Lang Syne, take hands from London to the Line!

    Good Luck to those that toiled with us since the days of Auld Lang Syne.

III.

Again, to all we hold most dear in life we left behind—

The wives we wooed, the bairns we kissed—and the loves of Auld Lang Syne.

    For surely, you'll have your sweetheart, and surely I have mine,

    We toast her name in silence here and the girls of Auld Lang Syne.

IV.

And last to him, the little man who led our fighting line

From Kabul on to Kandahar in the days of Auld Lang Syne.

    For Auld Lang Syne, and Bobs, our chief of Auld Lang Syne,

    We're here to do his work again as we did in Auld Lang Syne.

THE BOER WAR

(1900–1901)

Let us admit it fairly, as a business people should,
We have had no end of a lesson: it will do us no end of good...

—"THE LESSON 1899–1902 (BOER WAR)"

The Kipling family sailed for South Africa in January 1900 to spend the winter in Cape Town. In February, with a pass from Lord Frederick Roberts, commander of the British forces in the Boer War, Kipling visited the front at Paardeberg. On 21 March he joined the staff of *The Friend,* a newspaper taken over by the Army in Bloemfontein, capital of the Orange Free State; he copy-edited, corrected proofs, and wrote fables and poems for a run of twenty-six issues. The bound volume shown here was once in the files of A. P. Watt, Kipling's literary agent, with the author's anonymous articles authenticated thirteen times by his signature. Many of these contributions were later collected in *War's Brighter Side* by Julian Ralph, an American and fellow reporter on *The Friend.* Ralph included a portrait of Kipling from artist Mortimer Menpes's *War Impressions.*

Before leaving South Africa, Kipling composed a poem to the melody of "Auld Lang Syne," beginning "Be welcome to our hearts to-night," published as a fund-raising broadside at a Bloemfontein concert to benefit military widows and orphans held 18 April 1900. Other examples of his South African literary work were subject to pirate publication in faraway locales. The newspaper sketches "With Number Three" and "Surgical and Medical" were published with three uncollected poems in Santiago, Chile in 1900 by a Kipling admirer who owned a bookstore (and who later pulped or burned the unsold copies). "Be Welcome To Our Hearts Tonight" was included (as "Kipling's Auld Lang Syne") in a concert program in San Francisco, California, on 24 May 1900 (Queen Victoria's birthday), preceding even the first American newspaper appearance of the verses in *The New York Tribune* on 28 May. The author's most famous poem of the Boer War, "The Absent-Minded Beggar," is explored separately in this exhibition.

KIM

RUDYARD
KIPLING

Six Shillings

KIM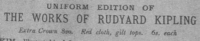

RUDYARD KIPLING

KIM

(1901)

Much I owe to the Lands that grew – | More to the Lives that fed –
But most to Allah who gave me two | Separate sides to my head.

—"THE TWO-SIDED MAN," KIM

Considered to be Kipling's greatest prose work, and the finest novel about the India of the British Empire, *Kim* first appeared in the United States in *McClure's Magazine* from December 1900 through October 1901 (S. S. McClure paid $25,000 for the serialization rights). The English magazine publication was in *Cassell's*, from January through November 1901. The book's ten plates of illustrations were photographs of bas-relief sculptures by the author's father Lockwood Kipling. The Canadian edition was made up from the U.S. sheets, and the cover of the paperback reproduced the frontispiece plate, Kim mounted on the cannon Zam-Zammah, the great gun of 1751, which stood on a raised platform outside the Lahore Museum where Lockwood was curator.

Delayed until the magazine appearances were virtually complete, the First English Edition was published on 17 October 1901, sixteen days after the First (American) Edition, in a first printing of 35,000 copies. The publisher Macmillan employed the same sheets, slightly trimmed, for the Colonial Library Edition, "intended for circulation only in India and the British Colonies," in both hardback and paperback, in 15,000 copies. Kipling presented the manuscript to the British Library in 1925.

THE JUST SO STORIES

(1902–1903)

I keep six honest serving men | (They taught me all I know);
Their names are What and Why and When | And How and Where and Who.
—"THE ELEPHANT'S CHILD"

ITEMS ON EXHIBIT

The Beginning of the Armadillos. [First (American copyright) Edition] (Philadelphia: 1900). One of twenty-five copies.

"How the Whale Got His Tiny Throat," *St. Nicholas*, December 1897.

"The Crab That Made the Tides," *Pearson's Magazine,* August 1902.

Just So Stories For Little Children. [First (English) Edition] (London: 1902). **[Ill. p. 68]**

The Just So Song Book. [First (English) Edition] (London: 1903). **[Ill. p. 70–71]**

The Just So Painting Books for Children (No. 3): How The Rhinoceros Got His Skin. ([First (English) Edition] (London: 1922)

The very first of these stories to appear in print, "How the Whale Got His Tiny Throat," in *St. Nicholas* for December 1897, featured an introductory paragraph noting that these stories "had to be told just so." When the First (English) Edition of *The Just So Stories* appeared on 30 September 1902, all of the twelve tales but one had appeared in American and English magazines between 1897 and 1902. Three of them ("The Elephant's Child," The Beginning of the Armadillos," and "The Sing-Song of Old Man Kangaroo") had also been printed separately for copyright protection in New York in 1900 by Kipling's London agent A. P. Watt. The cover design, the twenty-two full page black-and-white plates, and the chapter introductory initials are all by Kipling, drawn during the family winter in Cape Town in 1900–1901. This is his only self-illustrated trade publication.

To achieve simultaneous publication with the First American Edition, proofs of the English Edition were sent to Doubleday in New York. The book's untitled poems, which had not appeared in the magazine articles, were set to music in 1903 by Edward German in *The Just So Song Book*. In 1922, four of the stories were turned into watercolor painting books for children, published in both England and the United States.

39

VIII.
OF ALL THE TRIBE OF TEGUMAI.

Rudyard Kipling.　　　　　　　　　Edward German.

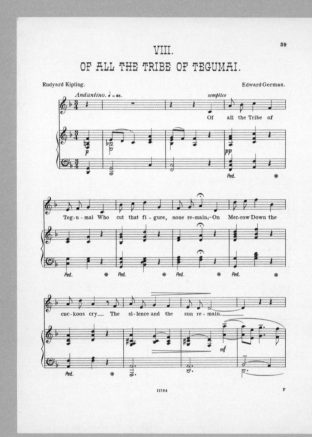

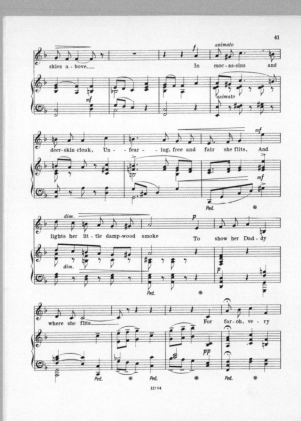

The Coin Speaks

Singers sing for Coin: but I,
Struck in Rome's last agony,
Shut the lips of Melody.

Many years my thin white face
Peered in every market-place
At the Doomed Imperial Race

Warmed against and worn between
Hearts uncleansed and hands unclean —
What is there I have not seen?

Not an Empire dazed and old —
Smitten blind and stricken cold —
Bartering her sons for gold.

Not the Plebs her rulers please
From the public Treasuries
With the bread and circuses

PUCK OF POOK'S HILL

Not her hard-won fields restored,
on the egregious Senate's word,
To the savage and the Sword.

Not the People's God-like Voice
As it welcomes or destroys
Month-old Idols of its choice

Not the Legions they disband,
Not the oar-less ships unmanned,
Not the ruin of the land:
These I know and understand:

ENGLAND REDISCOVERED

(1904–1911)

I am slowly discovering England, which is the most wonderful foreign land I have ever been in.
—LETTER TO H. RIDER HAGGARD

In 1902, the Kipling family moved to their last home, Bateman's, an ironmasters's house built in 1634 in Burwash, Sussex. After publishing his poetry collection *The Five Nations* (1903), Kipling turned his attention to the British past and landscape. *Traffics and Discoveries* appeared in October 1904. *Puck of Pook's Hill*, with ten stories and sixteen poems reflecting England's invasions by the Romans and the Danes, was published in October 1906; its American edition featured illustrations by Arthur Rackham (1867–1939), the artist's only work done for a Kipling book.

In June 1907, Kipling was awarded an honorary degree at Oxford, along with Samuel Clemens (Mark Twain), and in November of that year, became the first English author to be awarded the Nobel Prize for literature. *Actions and Reactions* appeared in October 1909, followed by the continuation of the Puck stories, *Rewards and Fairies* of October 1910. The latter's immensely popular poem "If—" received its own separate edition in America. His poem "The Female of the Species" was a reaction to the suffragist movement.

**Christmas
Greetings**
1914

To –

dear Eleanor & Franklin

With our love –

Maude – David

THE GREAT WAR–I
(1914–1915)

Once more we hear the word | That sickened earth of old: –
"No law except the Sword | Unsheathed and uncontrolled."
—"FOR ALL WE HAVE AND ARE"

With the coming of the First World War in August 1914, Kipling (who had predicted and even named "the Great War" as far back as 1899, and first damned "the shameless Hun" in his poem "The Rowers" that year) turned his heart, voice, and pen to the battle. His poem "For All We Have and Are" was printed in *The Times* on 2 September 1914, and promptly issued separately by Methuen. (The poem's first—and unauthorized—American edition was a Christmas 1914 keepsake printed by Eleanor Roosevelt's aunt.)

In *France at War* (October 1915), the author celebrated the pluck of a country he had loved since a boy, and in *The Fringes of the Fleet* (December 1915), the contributions of the auxiliary craft and submarines which supported the British fleet. The Hearst newspapers here reprinted the latter as *Rudyard Kipling With The British Fleet*, and distributed it to their readers in New York, Boston, Los Angeles, and San Francisco as a pamphlet with city-specific paper covers. Kipling often visited the Royal Navy's Eighth Submarine Flotilla, and wrote poems for *The Maidstone Magazine*, published by the crew of the H.M.S. *Maidstone*, a support ship headquartered in Harwich.

"THE TRADE."

THEY bear, in place of classic names,
    Letters and numbers on their skin.
They play their grisly blindfold games
    In little boxes made of tin.
    Sometimes they stalk a Zeppelin,
Sometimes they learn where mines are laid,
    Or where the Baltic ice is thin.
That is the custom of " the Trade."

Few prize-courts sit upon their claims.
    They seldom tow their targets in.
They follow certain secret aims
    Down under, far from strife or din.
    When they are ready to begin
No flag is flown, no fuss is made,
    More than the shearing of a pin.
That is the custom of " the Trade."

The Scout's quadruple funnel flames
    A mark from Sweden to the Swin,
The Cruiser's thund'rous screw proclaims
    Her comings out and goings in.
    But only whiffs of paraffin
Or creamy rings that fizz and fade
    Show where the one-eyed Death has been.
That is the custom of " the Trade."

viii

Their feats, their fortunes, and their fames
    Are hidden from their nearest kin;
No eager public backs or blames,
    No journal prints the yarns they spin
    Above the bitters and the gin
When they return from run or raid.
    Unheard they work, unseen they win.
That is the custom of "the Trade."

L'ENVOI.

Even the "Maidstone Magazine,"
    For whom my ribald rhymes are made,
Strikes out far more than it sticks in.
    That is the custom of "the Trade."

RUDYARD KIPLING.

To
Fighting Americans
by

Rudyard Kipling

AMERICAN EXPEDITIONARY FORCES
Young Men's Christian Association
in the United Kingdom.
12, Rue d'Aguesseau. Paris.

THE GREAT WAR–II
(1916–1918)

They shall not return to us, the resolute, the young,
The eager and whole-hearted whom we gave.
—"MESOPOTAMIA"

ITEMS ON EXHIBIT

Tales of "The Trade". [First (English) Edition] (London: 9 July 1916). One of twenty-five copies.

The Neutral. [First (American copyright) Edition] (New York: 29 November 1916). One of 100 copies.

To Fighting Americans. [First (English) edition] (London: September 1918). 50,000 copies printed; one of four known copies. [Ill. p. 78]

Kipling's Message. [First (English) Edition] (London: February 1918)

Kipling's Message. [First French Edition, for the American Y.M.C.A.] (Paris: 1918)

Every Ounce In Us. [First American Edition] (St. Louis?: 1918). The "Kipling's Message" speech, published by the Simmons Hardware Company of St. Louis, Missouri. The only known copy. [Ill. p. 80–81]

The Irish Guards. [First (English) Edition/Autograph Edition] (London: March 1918). One of 100 copies signed by Kipling.

Justice. [First English Edition] (London: January 1918).

In June 1916 Kipling's series of articles entitled *Tales of "The Trade"* appeared in *The Times* and other English newspapers, based on secret reports to the British Admiralty made available to the author for review. Clement King Shorter, a journalist, was given permission by the Admiralty (which held the copyright for the duration of the war) to reprint the three articles in a limited edition.

Kipling was frustrated by the refusal of the United States to enter the conflict, as his 1916 poem "The Neutral" made plain. When American troops were finally "over there," bivouacked in England, he spoke to them: *To Fighting Americans*, a pamphlet printed in London for the American Y.M.C.A. in Paris, contains two speeches made at the opening of an American officers' rest camp at Winchester, England, on 20 July 1918. An earlier speech, given at Folkestone on 15 February 1918, was published in London that month, reprinted the same month by the American Y.M.C.A. in Paris for free distribution to the troops, and then reprinted once more in the United States by a St. Louis hardware company in its series of patriotic pamphlets.

Kipling had secured a commission in the Irish Guards for his son John, who was reported missing at the Battle of Loos on 27 September 1915 (his body was never found). For a London benefit for the Guards on 18 March 1918, Kipling wrote the poem "The Irish Guards," and autographed 100 copies of a limited edition. "Justice," demanding as the Great War ended that Germany relearn the laws of civilization, appeared in 200 newspapers around the world in October and November 1918, and was published as a broadside in London.

RUDYARD KIPLING

Rudyard Kipling, was born at Bombay, India on December the thirtieth, 1865. He is the son of John Lockwood Kipling, who was an Architectural Sculptor at the Bombay School of Art for many years.

At the age of five, he came over from India and dwelled in Southsea, England, then went to the United Services College. While there he edited a school paper and contributed to a North Devon Journal.

While just a boy he penned many sonnets and poems, among them one entitled "The World," which was the first piece for which he received money.

At the age of sixteen, he returned to India and engaged in writing on the staff of "The Civil and Military Gazette" at Labore.

When eighteen years of age, he had produced a tiny volume of parodies called "Echoes." Later he became special correspondent to "The Pioneer" of Allahabad.

Between 1885 and 1898, he had published twenty-eight volumes of work and over a hundred stories, besides numerous poems.

Kipling traveled all over the world and wherever he was he wrote a story or poem about the country in which he was traveling or the place where he was stopping.

Rudyard Kipling, England's greatest novelist, ranks with Carlyle and the French, Hugo.

Every Ounce In Us

A Speech by Rudyard Kipling

I will tell you a story. Once upon a time, a hundred years ago, there was a large and highly organized community in India who lived by assassination and robbery. They were educated to it from their infancy; they followed it as a profession, and it was also their religion. They were called Thugs. Their method was to disguise themselves as pilgrims, or travelers, or merchants, and to join with parties of pilgrims, travelers and merchants moving about India. They got into the confidence of their victims, found out what they had on them, and in due time— after weeks or months of acquaintance—they killed them by giving them poisoned foods—sweetmeats for choice— or by strangling them from behind as they sat over the fire of an evening with a knotted towel or a specially prepared piece of rope.

Then they stripped the corpse of all valuables, threw it down a well or buried it, and went on to the next job.

The world has progressed since that day. By present standards of crime those thugs were ineffective amateurs.

They did not mutilate or defile the bodies of the dead; they did not torture or rape, or enslave people; they did not kill children for fun, and they did not burn villages.

They merely killed and robbed in an unobstructive way, as a matter of education, duty and religion, under the patronage of their Goddess, Kali the Destroyer. Very good.

At the present moment all the Powers of the World that have not been bullied or bribed to keep out of it have been forced to join in one international depart-

THE
YEARS BETWEEN

BY
RUDYARD KIPLING

METHUEN & CO. LTD., LONDON

THE POST WAR YEARS–I

(1918–1921)

Though all which once was England stands / Subservient to Our will,
The Dead of whom we washed Our Hands / They have observance still.
—"MEMORIES"

ITEMS ON EXHIBIT

Twenty Poems. [First (English) Edition] (London: May 1918).

Kipling-corrected type-scripts for *Twenty Poems*: "The Sons of Martha" and "The Holy War."

The Years Between. [First (English) Edition] (London: April 1919). [Ill. p. 82]

Autograph Manuscript, unsigned, "Gehazi" (October ? 1913). [Ill. p. 84–85]

Tours of the Battlefields of Belgium and France. [Third (English) Edition] (London: 1920). Only known copy.

Twenty Poems, appearing in May 1918, collected three poems for the first time, "The Sons of Martha," "For All We Have and Are," and "The Holy War" (although each had previously appeared in periodicals or separate editions). The title of *The Years Between*, published in April 1919, seemingly referred to the moral and political chaos of the two decades from the onset of the Boer War to the end to the Great War. It included one of the greatest of all hymns of hate, "Gehazi," Kipling's savage attack on Rufus Isaacs, who was appointed Lord Chief Justice of England despite his involvement in the Marconi insider trading scandal of 1913. The unnamed Isaacs is likened to the Old Testament servant in the Second Book of Kings, who was punished with leprosy for embezzlement.

Kipling had been appointed to the Imperial War Graves Commission, established to oversee the burial and commemoration of the war dead of the British Empire. He wrote much of the Commission's pamphlet, *The Graves of the Fallen*, as well as inscriptions for the cemeteries (for the unknowns: "A Soldier of the Great War known unto God"). When travel agency Thos. Cook & Sons began to organize cheap three-day visits to the French and Belgian battlefields, Kipling contributed a preface to the sales brochure about decorum for the tourist.

Gehazi
=

"Whence comest thou, Gehazi,
So reverend to behold,
In scarlet and in ermines
And chain of England's gold?"
"From following after Naaman
To tell him all is well,
Whereby my zeal hath made me
A Judge in Israel.

Well done, well done
~~with~~ Gehazi!
Stretch forth thy ready hand,
Thou barely 'scaped from judgment
to take oath to judge the land.
Unswayed by gift of money
Or privy bribe, more base,
Of knowledge which is profit
In any market-place.

To Search out & probe, Gehazi
~~Of~~ only thou canst try,
The ~~trustf~~ truthful well-weighed answer

To overbear a witness
  And make the Court keep still.

Take order now, Gehazi
  That no man talk aside
In secret with his judges
  The while his case is tried
Lest he should show them – reason
  To a matter hid
And subtly lead the question
  Away from what he did.

Thou mirror of uprightness,
  What ails thee at thy vows
What means the risen whiteness
  Of the skin between thy brows.
The boils that shine & burrow
  The sores that slough and bleed
The leprosy of Naaman
  On thee and all thy seed.

Stand up, stand up, Gehazi
  Draw close thy robe & go
Gehazi, judge in Israel
  A leper white as snow

LONDON STONE.

When you come to London Town,
       (Grieving--grieving!)
Bring your flowers and lay them down
       At the Place of Grieving.

When you come to London Stone,
       (Grieving--grieving!)
Bow your head and mourn your own,
       With ~~all~~ the others grieving.

For those minutes, let it wake--
       (Grieving--grieving!)
All the empty-heart and ache
       That isn't cured by grieving.

For those minutes, tell no lie:-
       (Grieving--grieving!)
"Grave, this is thy victory;
       And the sting of Death is grieving."

Where's our help, from Earth or Heaven,?
       (Grieving--grieving!)
To comfort us for what we've given,
       And only gained the grieving.

Heaven's too far and Earth too near,
       (Grieving--grieving!)
But our neighbour's standing here,
       Grieving as we're grieving.

What's his burden every day?
       (Grieving--grieving!)
Nothing man can count or weigh,
       But loss and Love's own grieving.

What's the tie betwixt us two
       (Grieving--grieving!)
That must last our whole lives through?
"As I suffer so do you."
       That may ease the grieving.

Rudyard Kipling

THE POST WAR YEARS—II

(1922–1932)

The Gods that are wiser than Learning | But kinder than Life have made sure
No mortal may boast in the morning | That even will find him secure.
—"A RECTOR'S MEMORY"

ITEMS ON EXHIBIT

Press photograph of Kipling at his installation as Rector of St. Andrew's University on 11 October 1923 (his cousin, Prime Minister Stanley Baldwin, stands to the left of Kipling).

Independence. [First (English) Edition] (London: 1923). Sir Edmund Gosse's copy.

London Town. [First (American intended copyright) Edition] (New York: 1923). One of approximately 100 copies.

London Stone. [First (American copyright) Edition] (New York: 1923). One of three known copies (the others are the Library of Congress copy and the publisher Doubleday's copy).

"London Stone", Kipling-corrected typescript.
[Ill. p. 86]

Debits and Credits [First (English) Edition] (London: 14 September 1926).

Limits and Renewals. [First American Edition] (New York: 1932). One of 204 copies signed by Kipling.

Kipling's poem "London Stone," an elegy on grieving for the dead, appeared in *The Times* (London) on November 10, 1923 (the eve of the fifth anniversary of Armistice Day). The American Sunday newspapers ran it under the title "London Town," and so the Doubleday firm, charged with producing pamphlet versions of Kipling's short works to preserve American copyright, ended up printing it under both titles.

In October 1923, Kipling was made Rector of St. Andrew's University in Scotland; his address "Independence" was promptly published in England and the United States. Kipling's last two major short story collections, in his signature combination of tales and poems, appeared in these years: *Debits and Credits* in September 1926, and *Limits and Renewals* in April 1932. His collection of speeches, *A Book of Words*, discussed elsewhere in this exhibition, was published in March 1928.

WESTMINSTER ABBEY

S. TRANSEPT

FUNERAL SERVICE

OF

RUDYARD KIPLING

Thursday, the 23rd January, 1936, at 12 noon

Entrance by West Cloister Door,   W. FOXLEY NORRIS,
    via Dean's Yard   Dean

TICKET HOLDERS ARE REQUESTED TO BE IN THEIR SEATS BY **11.45** A.M.

THE GATHERING STORM AND DEATH

(1932–1936)

We know that Ones and Ones make Twos – | Till Demos votes them Three or Nought.
We know the Fenris Wolf is loose. | We know the Fight has not been fought.
—"'BONFIRES ON THE ICE"

Like Churchill and a few other political observers, Kipling saw the rise of Hitler as an imminent threat. In the poem "The Storm Cone" of May 1932, published two weeks before the Nazi Party gained 230 seats in the Reichstag, he warned: "This is the tempest long foretold— | Slow to make head, but sure to hold." In his final verse statement on Germany, "Bonfires on the Ice," printed the day after the plebiscite in Germany which supported Hitler's decision to withdraw from the League of Nations, he warned against policies built on falsehood, cheering for a time, but in the end falling through their foundations. He also watched in dismay as the Aryan good luck symbol he had adopted for his books' decoration in 1899—the swastika—became the perverted symbol of a different order, and promptly ordered its removal from his bindings.

In March 1935 he published "Hymn of the Breaking Strain," a prayer for help from a mysterious God for delivery from the future hour "of overthrow and pain," and a personal meditation on his own physical collapse (he had been diagnosed with a duodenal ulcer in May 1933). The condition finally killed him on 18 January 1936. Two days later King George V died. "The King has gone," it was said, "and taken his trumpeter with him." Kipling's ashes were buried at Poets' Corner in Westminster Abbey on 23 January 1936, and the pallbearers included the Prime Minister, a Field Marshal, an Admiral of the Fleet, the Master of Cambridge's Magdalene College, the head of the Imperial War Graves Commission, Kipling's fellow Boer War reporter H. A. Gwynne, and his literary agent A. S. Watt. The service's concluding hymn, for the bard of Empire, was "Recessional."

Westminster Abbey

ORDER OF SERVICE

AT THE BURIAL

OF

RUDYARD KIPLING

ON

THURSDAY, JANUARY 23rd, 1936

AT 12 NOON

✠

[SUPPLEMENT TO THE ENGINEER, MARCH 15, 1935.]

Hymn of Breaking Strain

The careful text-books measure
   (Let all who build beware !)
The load, the shock, the pressure
   Material can bear.
So, when the faulty girder
   Lets down the grinding span,
The blame of loss, or murder,
   Is laid upon the man.
      Not on the Stuff—the Man!

But, in our daily dealing
   With stone and steel, we find
The Gods have no such feeling
   Of justice toward mankind.
To no set gauge they make us,—
   For no laid course prepare—
And presently o'ertake us
   With loads we cannot bear:
      Too merciless to bear!

The prudent text-books give it
   In tables at the end—
The stress that shears a rivet
   Or makes a tie-bar bend—
What traffic wrecks macadam—
   What concrete should endure—
But we, poor Sons of Adam,
   Have no such literature,
      To warn us or make sure!

We hold all earth to plunder—
   All Time and Space as well—
Too wonder-stale to wonder
   At each new miracle ;
Till, in the mid-illusion
   Of Godhead 'neath our hand,
Falls multiplied confusion
   On all we did and planned—
      The mighty works we planned.

We only, of Creation
   (Ah luckier bridge and rail !)
Abide the twin-damnation—
   To fail and know we fail.
Yet we—by which sole token
   We know we once were Gods—
Take shame in being broken
   However great the odds—
      The burden or the odds.

Oh veiled and secret Power
   Whose paths we search in vain,
Be with us in our hour
   Of overthrow and pain ;
That we—by which sure token
   We know Thy ways are true—
In spite of being broken—
   Because of being broken—
      May rise and build anew.
      Stand up and build anew!

         RUDYARD KIPLING.

honour of publishing for the first time one of his poems. It is fitting that we should recall another ... out of which trouble, and in response to the demand, the Government imposed duties and ... turning to the Government, in all countries, to protect it from harm.

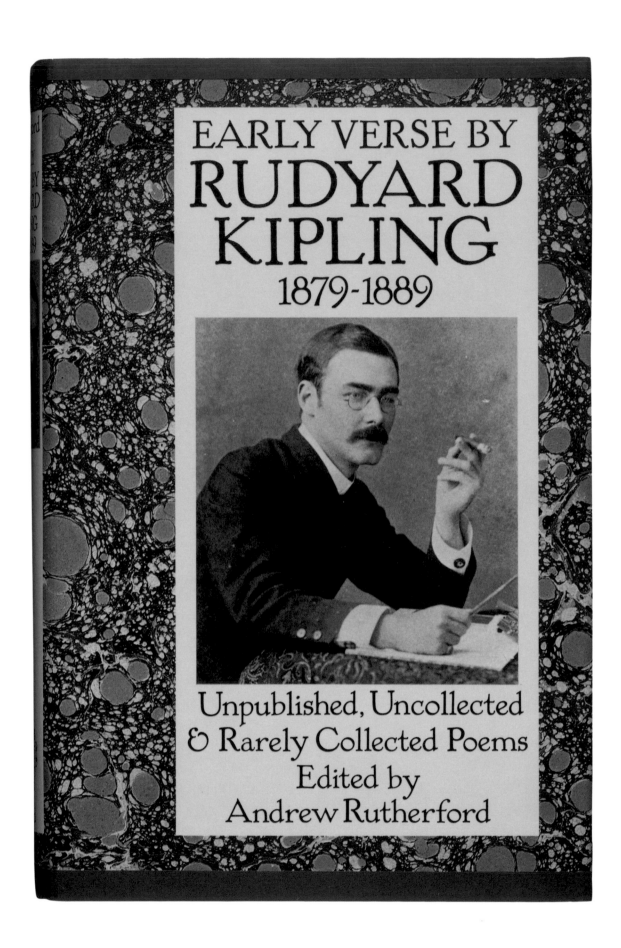

EARLY VERSE BY RUDYARD KIPLING 1879-1889

Unpublished, Uncollected & Rarely Collected Poems

Edited by Andrew Rutherford

MODERN FIRST EDITIONS

(1982–2005)

First editions of Kipling's works continue to be published to the present day, including collections of his earliest unpublished poems, his Indian journalism, his Japanese letters of travel, his life-long observations on the writer's craft, and a six-volume selection of his letters (1,888, from over 7,000 known). A complete edition of all his poems, expected to run up to four volumes, is planned by the Cambridge University Press.

KIPLING'S JAPAN
Collected Writings   Edited by
Hugh Cortazzi & George Webb

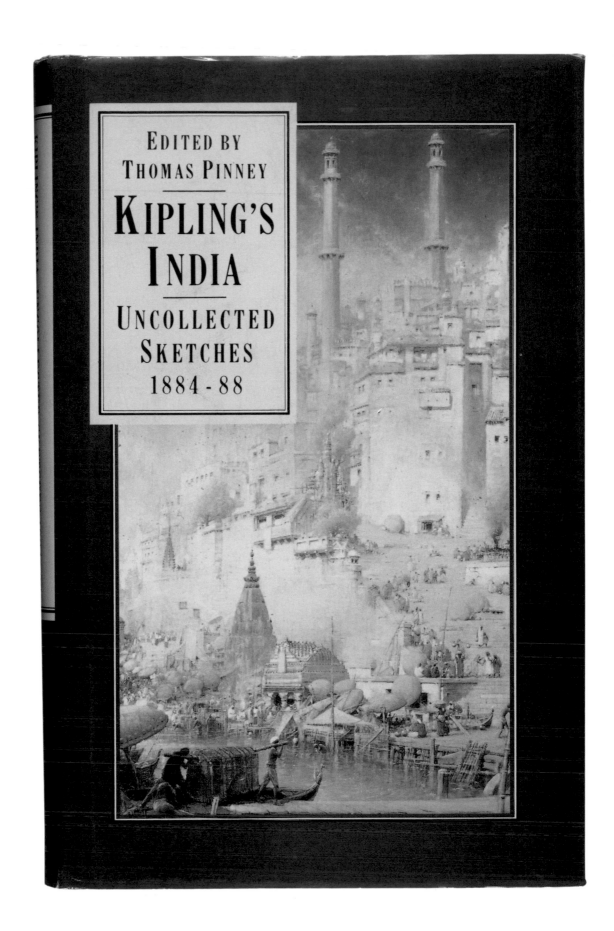

EDITED BY
THOMAS PINNEY

KIPLING'S
INDIA

UNCOLLECTED
SKETCHES
1884 - 88

THE ABSENT-MINDED BEGGAR ❧

· BY ·

RUDYARD KIPLING.

THE ABSENT MINDED BEGGAR
(1899)

Will you kindly drop a penny in my little tambourine
For a gentleman in kharki ordered South?
—"THE ABSENT-MINDED BEGGAR"

ITEMS ON EXHIBIT

'Rudyard Kipling's New Poem The Absent Minded Beggar' [First Appearance] *The Daily Mail,* 31 October 1899.

The Absent-Minded Beggar. [First (English) Illustrated 'Art' Edition] (London: 1899). The special satin Lillie Langtry recital issue. **[Ill. p. 96]**

The Absent-Minded Beggar. [First musical edition, first issue] (London: 25 November 1899).

The Absent-Minded Beggar. [First Canadian Edition] (Montreal: 1899).

The Absent-Minded Beggar. [First American Edition] (New York: February 1890).

The Absent-Minded Beggar. [Cigarette Box Edition] (London: 1899).

Tea Set (tray, teapot, creamer and sugar bowl). Macintyre, Burslem, England [1904–1913] **[Ill. p. 98–99]**

Canister cup and saucer. Macintyre, Burslem, England [1904–1913]

A Gentleman in Kharki brass trivet with Caton Woodville figure. England, [1900?]

The Boer War began on 12 October 1899. Kipling turned down an offer from the proprietor of *The Daily Mail* to be a war correspondent, but agreed to assist in raising money for the newspaper's "Soldiers' Families Fund" to buy tobacco, soap and cocoa for the troops, and clothing and postage for food parcels for their dependents. "The Absent-Minded Beggar" appeared in *The Daily Mail* on 31 October 1899, and with Kipling's blessing, the newspaper published and sold various editions of its own and licensed it to others, for a contribution to the Fund, which by 1903 had raised £340,000 (over $20,000,000 in present day value).

The newspaper's illustrated edition, featuring a sepia drawing of "a gentleman in *kharki*" by celebrated war artist R. Caton Woodville, was sold in paper and white satin triptych form, with the poem in holograph facsimile; a special issue was printed for the actress Lillie Langtry's recital at the Garrick Theatre. *The Daily Mail* also issued a damask cotton, color illustrated edition. Composer Arthur Sullivan set the verses to a melody that Kipling noted approvingly in his autobiography was "guaranteed to pull teeth out of barrel-organs." The First Canadian Edition was a "Patriotic Envelope," and the First South African Edition a broadside, autographed by Kipling for a charity auction before he left Cape Town after editing *The Friend.* There were Absent-Minded Beggar cigarettes, which came with their own miniature pamphlet of the poem. In William Moorcroft's Macintyre pottery in Burslem, England, the holograph and the Woodville drawing were transferred onto teapots, cups and saucers, wine jugs, pitchers, candy dishes, match strikers, and other china objects.

The Absent-minded Beggar

When you've shouted "Rule Britannia" – when you've sung "God Save the Queen"
When you've finished killing Kruger with your mouth –
Will you kindly drop a shilling in my little tambourine
For a gentleman in kharki ordered South?
He's an absent-minded beggar and his weaknesses are great –
But we and Paul must take him as we find him –
He is out on active service, wiping something off a slate –
And he's left a lot of little things behind him!

OLD JOHNNY GRUNDY.

Old Johnny Grundy had a Grey Mare.
  Hey! Gee! Whoa!

Her legs were thin & her hide was bare
  Hey! Gee! Whoa!

And when she died she made her Will:—
" Now old Johnny Grundy has used me ill;

" Give every dog in the Town a bone,
" But to old Johnny Grundy give thou none."

The Carver came and her image made
  In the Market-place where the Children played

And the Parson preached with unction rare:—
" Good people be kind to your old Grey Mare.

" And dont you beat her or use her ill
  Hey! Gee! Whoa!
" Or else she'll leave you out of her Will."
  Hey! Gee! Whoa!

Rudyard Kipling

CHARITY FUNDRAISING BOOKS

(1892–1935)

Kipling was always prepared to contribute stories or tales to collections published to raise funds for charity, and the selection here is a representative but small sample of his range of contributions over the years (most of which became first editions of his work). Kipling submitted "Old Johnny Grundy" to *Fame's Tribute To Children*, organized to benefit a children's day care center for the Columbian Exposition of 1893 in Chicago. He composed "Romance" for *Under Lochnagar*, an 1894 collection to benefit Queen Victoria's parish church in Balmoral, Scotland. His Shakespeare parody about automobiles, "The Marrèd Drives of Windsor," first appeared in *The Flag*, sold by the Union Jack Club in 1908 to build London sleeping accommodations for servicemen. The verses "The Last of the Light Brigade" and "1857–1907" were included in *Our Veterans*, published for the Crimean and Indian Veterans' Association Bazaar of 1908.

The Legion Book, published in 1929 as a tribute to the patron of the British Legion, H.R.H. The Prince of Wales (later Edward VIII and, after his abdication, the Duke of Windsor), contained Kipling's poem "The English Way," and was sold in a trade edition and a 600-copy limited edition, of which 100 were printed on large paper for distribution by the prince himself with autographs of all 85 contributors (a virtual catalogue of the prominent authors and artists of that time).

The Pageant of Parliament, a program for the summer festival held in Albert Hall in the summer of 1934, contained three poems, two in Elizabethan language and the third, "Non Nobis Nomine," later set to music.

TO HIS

ROYAL HIGHNESS THE

PRINCE OF WALES, K.G.

SIR,

WE, WHOSE NAMES ARE SIGNED
OVERLEAF, CONTRIBUTORS AT
YOUR GRACIOUS INVITATION
TO THIS BOOK PUBLISHED IN
AID OF THE BRITISH LEGION,
BEG TO DEDICATE OUR WORK
TO YOUR ROYAL HIGHNESS,
PATRON OF THE LEGION

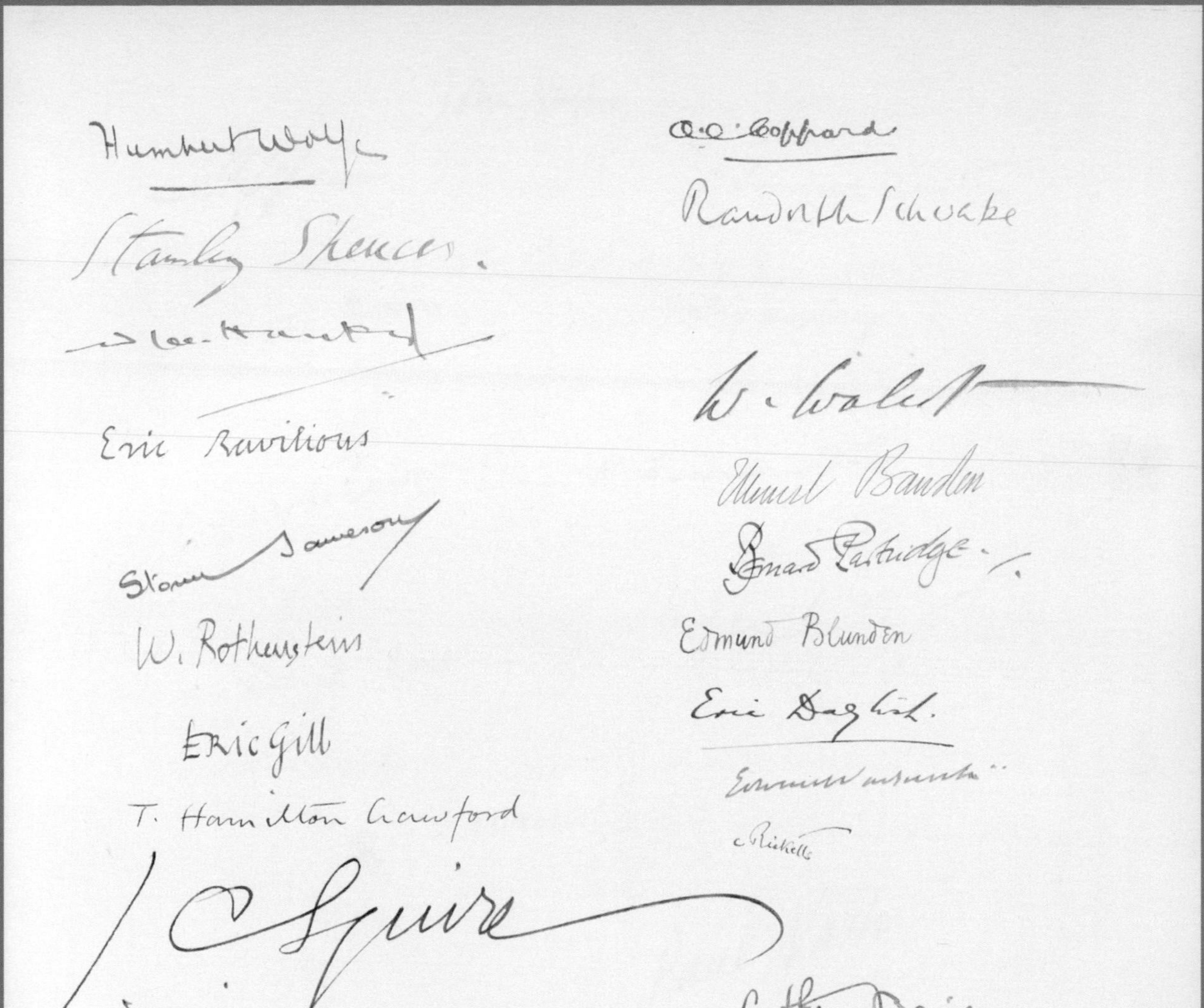
Humbert Wolfe
A. E. Coppard
Randolph Schwabe
Stanley Spencer
W. Walcot
Eric Ravilious
Edward Bawden
Storm Jameson
Bernard Partridge
W. Rothenstein
Edmund Blunden
Eric Gill
Eric Daglish
T. Hamilton Crawford
C. Ricketts
J. C. Squire
Arthur Briscoe
F. Dobson
William Orpen
Laura Knight
Laurence Binyon
John Galsworthy
W. Heath Robinson
Rudyard Kipling
Robert Bridges

RUDYARD KIPLING'S

INDICTMENT

OF

THE GOVERNMENT.

E. A. Hoppé

The famous speech at Tunbridge Wells on May 16th, 1914.

PUBLISHED BY

The Daily Express,

23, ST. BRIDE STREET, E.C.

PRICE ONE PENNY.

SPEECHES
(1907–1933)

Fiction is Truth's elder sister. Obviously.
No one in the world knew what truth was till somebody had told a story.
—"FICTION"

ITEMS ON EXHIBIT

Speech of Rudyard Kipling as Chairman at the Annual Dinner of the Artists' General Benevolent Institution, on May the Ninth, 1907. [First (English) Edition] (London: 1907). Collected in *A Book of Words* as "The Claims of Art."

Address by Rudyard Kipling to The Canadian Club. [First (Canadian) Edition] (Winnipeg: 1907). In the fall of 1907, Kipling toured across Canada, making a series of speeches to various city branches of The Canadian Club about the country's role and prospects in the British Empire. One of two known copies, the other being Kipling's copy now at Sussex University marked as copy text for "Growth and Responsibility" in *A Book of Words*.
[Ill. p. 107]

"Rudyard Kipling" by Richard Godard Mathews, drawn during Kipling's Canadian tour for the *Montreal Daily Star*, published 26 October 1907, signed by Mathews and autographed by Kipling.
[Ill. p. 106]

Doctors: An Address delivered to the Students of the Medical School of the Middlesex Hospital, 1st October 1908. [First (English) Edition] (London: 1908). Sold to benefit the hospital, in which Kipling was to die twenty-eight years later. Collected, as "A Doctor's Work," in *A Book of Words*.

Rudyard Kipling's Indictment of the Government. The Famous Speech at Tunbridge Wells on May 16th, 1914. [First (English) Edition] [London: 1914]. An attack on the government of Prime Minister Asquith and its Home Rule Bill for Ulster in northern Ireland, charging that the legislation was in exchange for passage of the Parliament Act to provide the first salary for its members.
[Ill. p. 104]

England and the English. Festival Dinner, the Royal Society of St. George, 23 April 1920. [Second English Edition] (London: 1920). Kipling was chairman for this dinner, held on the feast day of England's patron saint, and this edition was used to encourage application for membership in this society. Collected in *A Book of Words* under this title.

The King's Pilgrimage. [First (English) Edition] (London: 1922). Contains Kipling's speech written for delivery by King George V at Terlincthun Cemetery on 13 May 1922 during the visit of the king (and Kipling) to several of the war cemeteries of the British dead in France.

Report Of Speech By Mr. Rudyard Kipling, LL.D., at the Annual Dinner of the Chamber of Shipping of The United Kingdom Friday, 20th February 1925. [Second English and First Separate Edition] (London: 1925). Produced by the Chamber of Shipping in 22,000 copies for distribution to secondary schools through Great Britain; collected in *A Book of Words* as "Shipping."

The Art of Fiction. Issued by permission of The Times, in whose columns the report appeared on July 8, 1926. [First (English) Edition] (London: 1926). Speech to the Royal Society of Literature, in an unauthorized edition, cancelled at Kipling's direction (but copies survived, and this one he autographed, bemused by a portrait of him at age 34 used to illustrate a speech given when he was age 61). Collected in *A Book of Words* as "Fiction".

A Book of Words. Selections From Speeches and Addresses Delivered Between 1906 and 1927. [First (English) Edition] (London: 1928). Eighteen of these thirty-one addresses received their first book publication in this edition.

"Rhodes Scholars", in *The Living Age*, 5 July 1924. [First Magazine Appearance]. Delivered at Town Hall in Oxford, 6 June 1924, and collected in *A Book of Words* as "Work in the Future." Rudyard and Carrie Kipling has advised Cecil Rhodes in South Africa in 1902 on the establishment of the Rhodes Scholarships, and Rudyard served for eight years on the Rhodes Trust.

B.B.C. Year-Book 1934. [First (English) Edition] (London: 1933). Contains George V's first Christmas address to the Empire, broadcast over the B.B.C. on Christmas Day 1932, and written by Kipling without public acknowledgment.

Kipling was not shy about speaking on behalf of cultural or political causes in which he believed, as shown in the exhibition cases on the First World War. He was also often invited to speak to professional guilds and groups at their dinners, sometimes in connection with his being conferred honorary memberships in those organizations. His first known speech was to his Masonic Lodge in Lahore in 1887, when he was twenty-one, and his last was to Canadian schoolchildren at Eastbourne in 1935, when he was sixty-nine. In 1928, he collected several of his addresses in *A Book of Words*. He also wrote many speeches for King George V and other members of the royal family, but this was kept secret at the time.

Rudyard Kipling

R. J. Mathews

Address

BY

Rudyard Kipling

TO THE

Canadian Club

WINNIPEG

2ND OCTOBER, 1907

PRINTED BY

JACKSON ENGRAVING CO.

375 HARGRAVE ST.

These two letters were printed in the
Medicine Hat *News* for December 22, 1910
and they have again been put into type
At the Sign of The George
twelve years later as a slight contribution
to an effort to check the increasingly
widespread tendency toward
Universal Conformity.

PIRATED EDITIONS

(1891–1983)

ITEMS ON EXHIBIT

Kipling was engaged for much of his life in a war against "pirates," the term for publishers who print copies of works without permission. Kipling had no editorial control over pirated editions and he received no payment for them. Until passage of international copyright law in the United States with the Chase Act of July 1891, anyone in the U.S. could publish Kipling's writings, and even after the passage of the act, his pre-1891 titles were not protected. Kipling suppressed three separate book editions of collections of his work in India, and retained New York lawyer Augustus Gurlitz to commence a number of lawsuits in the United States to protect his literary intellectual property, most notably against G. P. Putnam's Sons, who published a "Brushwood Edition," which rivaled the authorized (and more expensive) "Outward Bound Edition" of his collected works published by Scribner's. Private press proprietors such as Fred Goudy, Carl Purington Rollins (later Printer to the Yale University Press), and George Parker Winship (Librarian at Harvard University) published limited, unauthorized editions, as did admirers, his personal physician, several collector-scholars, and even some university libraries.

The Courting of Dinah Shadd and Other Stories. [First (American) Edition, first issue] (New York: September 1890). Containing five stories first appearing in *Harper's Weekly,* but not authorized for book publication, and the first book to be published with Kipling's portrait.

Letters of Marque. [First (Indian) Edition] (Allahabad: 1891). Produced by the publisher of the Indian Railway Library titles, suppressed at Kipling's demand; one of 1,000 copies, 900 supposedly destroyed.
[Ill. p. 112]

American Notes. [First (American) Edition, first issue] (New York: 1891). Letters of travel about his 1889 tour across the United States, later edited by Kipling for authorized publication as *From Sea to Sea* in 1899; also the first book edition of Robert Louis Stevenson's *The Bottle Imp.*

"Bobs". [First (English) Edition] (London?: 1894?). Suppressed edition of the poem, first appearing in *Pall Mall Magazine* for December 1893; the only known copy.

The Dipsy Chanty. [First American Separate Edition] (East Aurora, NY: 1898). Published by Elbert Hubbard of the Roycroft Shop, who here retitled Kipling's 1893 poem "The Last Chantey" and published 950 copies. This is the trial exhibit copy used in the lawsuit by Kipling and his publisher Appleton, in successfully suing to seize all unsold copies.
[Ill. p. 113]

Mandalay. [First (American) Separate Edition] (New York: 1898). The New York publishing house of M. F. Mansfield made a specialty of pirate editions of Kipling, often illustrated as here by Blanche McManus.

The White Man's Burden. [First English Edition] (London: 1899). This, the source of one of Kipling's most famous phrases, is one of perhaps 100 copies produced by famed literary forger Thomas J. Wise, "printed for private circulation" just a week after the verses' newspaper appearance.

Explanation, Parody and Criticism of Rudyard Kipling's Celebrated Poem "The White Man's Burden". [First American trade edition, suppressed] (Chicago: March 1899). This "explanation" of the poem by a Chicago minister included the verses as copyrighted in the February 1899 *McClure's Magazine,* so Kipling sued, and the two leaves with his poem were torn out of all copies. One of three known intact survivors.
[Ill. p. 111]

The trial notebook of attorney Augustus Gurlitz in Kipling's lawsuit against G. H. Putnam's "Brushwood Edition" of Kipling's collected works, and Defendant's Exhibit No. 1, a prospectus for the Scribner's Outward Bound Edition.

Putnam. [First American Edition] (New York: 192?). In 1900 Kipling printed on a hand press the original of this savage attack on American publisher George Putnam, on brown toilet paper in two copies; this undated facsimile was made two decades later on white toilet paper by Max Harzof, owner of the G. A. Baker auction house.

The Gypsy Trail. [First (American) Edition] (Boston: 1904). This separate (and title-respelled) edition of Kipling's 1892 poem "The Gipsy Trail" was printed by Carl Purington Rollins (later Yale University Printer) for publisher Alfred Bartlett; the second edition, published in December 1905, was printed by Fred and Bertha Goudy at The Village Press (here in its limited edition of 39 copies).

Abaft the Funnel. [First (American) Edition] (New York: 11 October 1909). This collection of Kipling stories from *Turn-Overs* and the Indian newspapers *The Week's News* and *The Pioneer* was made up from typescripts by New York bookseller Luther Livingston and his wife Flora (later a Kipling bibliographer) and sold to publisher B. W. Dodge.

The Explorer. [First (American) Separate Edition] (Montague, MA: August 1911). Printed by Carl Purington Rollins at his Montague Press, the equipment of which was moved to New Haven to become the nucleus for the Yale University Press on Rollins's appointment as Printer to the University in 1920. The only known copy, of twenty-five printed.

Kipling's Advice to "The Hat." [First (American) Edition] (Dover, MA: 1 January 1923). Kipling's letter of advice to the town of Medicine Hat, Alberta, Canada, deploring the proposal to change its name; printed by Harvard College Librarian George Parker Winship, in two cover variants, for distribution within the circle of Kipling collectors.
[Ill. p. 108]

A Letter by Rudyard Kipling Concerning A Proposition to Buy the Cottage in Which Edgar Allan Poe Wrote ULLALUME. [First (American) Edition] (Chicago: 1924). Letter of 7 March 1896 printed by Kipling collector William H. Carpenter in about 200 copies; Carpenter's collection, including the original letter, is now in the Library of Congress.

Unpublished Items by Rudyard Kipling. [First (English) Edition] (London: 1943). Containing typescripts of Kipling's poems "The Burden of Jerusalem" and "A Chapter of Proverbs," printed by the deceased author's physician Alfred Webb-Johnson, then President of the Royal College of Surgeons, who made copies as gifts for Prime Minister Winston Churchill and, at Churchill's suggestion, for President Franklin D. Roosevelt. One of four known copies.

A Christmas Greeting. [First (London) Edition] (Mid-Atlantic Ocean: October 1965). Printed on shipboard by Kipling collector H. Dunscombe Colt on his way to the Kipling Society Centenary Luncheon, held 27 October 1965 in London, where the copies were distributed; the poem's fair copy is in the Colt Collection in the Library of Congress.

EXPLANATION, PARODY AND CRITICISM

OF

RUDYARD KIPLING'S

CELEBRATED POEM

"The White Man's Burden"

Published in McClure's Magazine for February.   Copyrighted by the author.

The Cream of the Daily Press Clippings

SINCE POEM APPEARED

COMPILED BY

F. B. WHIPPLE & CO., PRINTERS

308 DEARBORN STREET, CHICAGO

Circuit Court of the United States
Northern District of New York

Rudyard Kipling and D. Appleton
& Company   Complainants
against
Elbert Hubbard
Defendant.

In Equity.
No. 6760.

Complainants' Exhibit.
Defendant's Book. B.

STEAM TACTICS

By RUDYARD KIPLING

Price, Ten Cents

The Curtis
Publishing Company
Philadelphia, Pa.

COPYRIGHT EDITIONS
(1899–1944)

Promptly after adherence to international copyright law by the United States in July 1891, which required for valid American copyright that a work be printed in the United States and that two copies be deposited in the Library of Congress, Kipling arranged for the publication and nominal sale of special, limited-number copyright editions of his poems and stories here, prepared by his American magazine or book publishers to precede or coincide with the individual work's English periodical or book appearance. For this reason, first American editions of Kipling titles that are first calendar editions are more numerous than for any other author. There are 117 such American titles, in 134 separate pamphlet or broadside issues (plus 13 prepared in England between 1895 and 1912 at the instruction of Kipling's literary agent A. P. Watt). The numbers printed were often very small, and so no library, private or public, including the Library of Congress and the British Library, has a complete run of all the American and English copyright editions.

TALES
OF "THE TRADE"

I

SOME WORK IN THE BALTIC

TALES
OF "THE TRADE"

II

BUSINESS IN THE SEA OF MARMORA

TALES

III

RAVAGES AND REPAIRS

BY

RUDYARD KIPLING

THE BRITISH ADMIRALTY

places at the disposal of the Press of America
the following article, which has been written
from confidential reports in its possession
June, 1916.

GARDEN CITY   NEW YORK
DOUBLEDAY, PAGE & COMPANY
1916

ON

Dry=Cow Fishing

AS A FINE ART

BY

RUDYARD KIPLING

AUTHORIZED PRIVATE PRESS PRINTINGS AND MINIATURE BINDINGS

A Letter From Rudyard Kipling On A Possible Source Of The Tempest. [First (American) Edition] (Providence, RI: 1906). This letter, Kipling's meditation on Shakespeare's inspiration for *The Tempest,* stimulated by the author's visit to Bermuda in 1894, appeared in *The Spectator* for 2 July 1898. This edition was published with his permission by Edwin Collins Frost, the Shakespeare librarian for American collector Marsden Perry of Providence, in fifty-two copies distributed to friends, mostly college professors.

On Dry-Cow Fishing As A Fine Art. [First (American) Edition] (Cleveland, OH: 26 March 1926). This tale of how an angler hooked a cow first appeared in *The Fishing Gazette* for 13 December 1890. American bibliophile Paul Lemperley secured the author's blessing for a limited edition of 176 copies (6 went to Kipling), designed by Bruce Rogers, printed by William E. Rudge in Mt. Vernon, New York, and published by Lemperley's distinguished club of Cleveland book collectors, The Rowfant Club. [Ill. p. 118]

Why Snow Falls At Vernet. [First English Separate Edition] (London: 1963). This edition of a story, not collected by Kipling after its appearance in the magazine *The Merry Thought* in 1911, was published in an edition of fifty copies by American collector H. Dunscombe Colt and his wife Arvida, proprietors of the Two Horse Press, and distributed as a Christmas keepsake at a dinner of the Kipling Society in New York City in 1963.

The Neolithic Adventures of Taffi-Mai Metallu-Mai: How the First Letter Was Written and How the Alphabet Was Made. (Marina del Rey, CA: 1997). This edition of two of the Just So Stories by the Beiler Press in French-fold, side-stitched wraps in the Japanese style was published in an edition of 150 numbered copies.

With the Night Mail. (San Francisco: 1998). The Arion Press of San Francisco published Kipling's science fiction story of 1909 (set in the year 2000) in an edition of 250 copies, with illustrations by Victor Perez and introduction by Kipling scholar Thomas Pinney.

Some Kipling admirers and proprietors of private presses did seek permission from Kipling to print or reprint his work, and received it from the author or, after his death, from the executors of his literary estate (which benefits The National Trust of Great Britain, the owner, among other historic English properties, of Kipling's last home, Bateman's in Sussex).

The Princess and the Pickle Bottle. [First (American) Edition] (New York, NY: 2006). The first version of the story which became "The Potted Princess" when appearing in *St. Nicholas Magazine* for 1893, here printed in 100 hand-sewn, hand-numbered copies with reproductions of the author's drawings from the original manuscript, now at Beinecke Library. [Ill. p. 120–121]

Pearls From Kipling (New Britain, CT: 1963). One of 500 copies, lithographed at Connecticut State College for the Elihu Burritt Library.

How The Rhinoceros Got His Wrinkled Skin. (Southampton, MA: 1976). One of seventy-five copies on mulberry paper, signed by illustrator-publisher Sarah Chamberlain.

Kipling's American Catches. Epic Story of Heroic Size About Exploits in Salmon Fishing. (Berkeley, CA: 1980). One of 150 copies, on German Ingres antique paper, signed by J. R. Adams and printer Maryline P. Adams of The Poole Press.

The Elephant's Child, or How the Elephant Got His Trunk. (Berkeley, CA: 1990). One of 100 copies, on Basingwerk paper, signed by M. P. Adams of The Poole Press.

The Princess in the Pickle Bottle

RUDYARD KIPLING

The Princess in the Pickle-Bottle.

I

Once upon a time There was a Princess who lived in a Pickle-Bottle because Fairy-Land was full. Now There was only one way to get out of that Bottle and the King who was The Father of the Princess said that any one who rescued the Princess should first be compelled to marry her and secondly to govern half a Kingdom. As the princess was very beautiful and the Kingdom, was very large 10,764,302. Princes, all of Unblemished Reputation tried to open the Pickle-Bottle. 9,763,824. Princes consulted Court Magicians, Astrologers and Old Men whom they met in the Woods. 264,280 Princes took the advice of Fairy God mothers, While Witches, Magic Foxes, Enchanted Horses and Faithful Servants.

Consequently They Killed
10765 Red Dragons all supposed to guard the Pickle-Bottle

45689 Trolls,
1765 Dwergs
3764 Lame Dwarfs
189 One eyed Giants
} all supposed to guard the Pickle-Bottle.

And They said .846,729 Infallible Charms and Incantations any one of which was warranted to split Mountains of Glass and open the most Secret Treasures in all the World.

But the Pickle-Bottle would not open; and they all went away very Sorrowfully taking the heads of the Blue Dragons, and the Trolls and the Dwergs, and the Lame Dwarfs and the One-Eyed Giants along with them and looking back over Their Shoulders at the Princess in the Pickle-Bottle.

II

But there came along just One Prince and he was so poor that he could never afford to keep a Court Magician and his only Faithful Servants were his Two Hands. He walked on his feet because he had no horse to ride and he whistled as he walked.

When he came to the Pickle-Bottle he walked round it and nodded to the Princess inside and put his head askew and shut one eye and whistled as the other Princes told him about The Blue Dragons and the Dwergs and the charms that could not work. The Princess looked at him between her fingers and blushed for he was the Most Beautifullest of all the Princes

At last he put his hand into his pocket and said: " What is the matter with pulling out the Cork of this Pickle-Bottle?" And the other princes Said" Ah!" for they had not thought of that.

Then he pulled out the cork with a Corkscrew and it came out because it was just an ordinary cork in a common bottle which did not know anything about charms and Incantations. And the Princess came out of the bottle at the open end and all the Other princes cut off the heads of all the Court Magicians, Wizards, Witches, Faithful Servants, Talking Foxes and Enchanted Horses because they were annoyed.

And the Prince married the Princess and they lived happy ever after.

The Moral of this Story is: Next time you find a Princess in a Pickle-Bottle never try to open the Bottle with charms and Blue Dragons. Take a Corkscrew. Rudyard Kipling

Oct. 2. 99.

Dear Sir

In reply to yours of the 19th ult; the assortment of Kipling material which has been offered to you, is not sanctioned by me in any way whatever. You will observe that it includes matter which has been privately printed. It also includes matter which I have not written — as well as matter copyrighted in the United States of America.

Faithfully yours

Rudyard Kipling.

J. M. Wullesley

COLLECTED WORKS

(1897–1941)

As noted earlier in this catalogue, the first set of Kipling "collected works" was published by John W. Lovell in joining the "Indian Tales" and *Mine Own People* in a uniform binding in 1890–1891. The first clearly authorized collected edition to appear either in England or the United States was the Outward Bound Edition, conceived by Frank N. Doubleday in 1896 and published by Charles Scribner's Sons beginning in 1897. The price was $2 per volume, and the edition could only be purchased by subscription as an entire set. Other collected editions appeared over the years, aimed at different audiences and incomes, and culminating with the finally revised texts of the Sussex Edition, published in 1937–39, after Kipling's death, in 35 volumes and 525 sets (most destroyed unbound in the warehouse during the London Blitz of 1940–41). Its American counterpart was the Burwash Edition, with the same texts published by Doubleday, Doran in 1941.

To oblige a young American Lady.

The undersigned is guaranteed
by the writer to be one
of the ways in which it
is possible to write the name
Rudyard Kipling
It can also be written
Rudyard Kipling

P. 70

or otherwise:
Rudyard Kipling
or subsequently: —
Rudyard Kipling
or, for effect —
Rudyard Kipling
or lastly
Rudyard Kipling

KIPLINGIANA
(1899–1938)

Rudyard Kipling Bookmark Photograph. Produced by cigarette manufacturer John Player & Sons, Nottingham, 1899, in a series of ten which included Robert Louis Stevenson as No. 1, Kipling as No. 2, and Arthur Conan Doyle as No. 4.

Kipling Plug Cut. A tobacco tin from Louisville, Kentucky, contents intact, with internal government inspection strip dated June 1898.

A Kipling Calendar. (New York: 1898). Twelve drawings in color by Blanche McManus, published by M. F. Mansfield & Company, New York, containing excerpts from pre-1891 poems lacking American copyright protection; the front cover poem is by Edgar Wallace, missing one line from the original: "You're the poet of the cuss-word an' the swear."

The Kipling Guide Book. A Handy Guide to Rudyard Kipling's Life and Writings, With a Bibliography of His Works. (Birmingham, England, 1899).

Kipling Handbook. This novelty was issued as a single sheet, laid in the San Francisco newspaper *The Examiner* for 5 March 1899. Folded to thirty-two pages and fixed with a straight pin, it made a miniature book. All of its contents had been previously published.

The Rudyard Kipling Calendar. Published in London annually by G. Delgado, Ltd., from 1928 (for 1929) through 1938 (for 1939), with weekly leaves.
[Ill. p. 127]

Rudyard Kipling. [Cigarette Card] No. 81 in the General Interest series, Ogden's Guinea Gold Cigarettes (London: 1899).

Rudyard Kipling. [Cigarette Card] No. 90 in the Prominent People series, Scerri's High Class Cigarettes [Malta: 1930].

Rudyard Kipling. [Cigarette Card] No. 26 in the Builders of Empire series, J. Wix & Sons Ltd. (London: 1937).

Kipling Homme de Lettres. [Chocolate Card] 2e Collection, Felix Potin (Paris: 1899?).

Kipling's enormous popularity led to the appropriation of his image for advertising in predictable as well as unlikely ways. His writings were mined for aphorisms printed in calendars, with and without his permission, and "guides" to his work were prepared for the general reader who wanted to know more about the exotic settings of his poems and stories. As a celebrity, he maintained his good humor with admirers who sought his autograph and his advice.

Autograph Note Signed, undated, "To oblige a young American Lady" (presumably a child, and unidentified), Kipling signed his name six times, in six different ways.
[Ill. p. 124]

Autograph Letter Signed, Kipling's April 1910 letter to Charles Gallup, an American from Coxsackie, New York, responding to Gallup's second request for an autograph; with an engraved portrait of Kipling by T. Johnson, signed in pencil.
[Ill. p. 126]

⚓ BURWASH

🚂 ETCHINGHAM

BATEMAN'S
BURWASH
·SUSSEX·

Ap. 4. 1910

My dear Sir

I have just returned from
abroad to find your very kind
note of Mar. 3rd waiting for
me. I very much appreciate
the spirit in which you have
met my demand. You will
understand of course that people
who volunteer double what they
are asked are very rarely met
with — outside of a poker game
where. I understand, they do not play
for their health, or other peoples good.
I have never collected autographs
myself but as a steady and
delightful hobby I have gone in for
keeping bees and have had untold
interest and amusement out of it
with best wishes to yourself and
to Mrs Gallup believe me
                  very sincerely yours
                  Rudyard Kipling
                  _____

To
C. Gallup Esq

A KIPLING CALENDAR

With Twelve Drawings in color by Blanche McManus accompanying appropriate text from Barrack-Room Ballads and Departmental Ditties .. ..

RUDYARD KIPLING

" *You're our partic'lar author, you're our patron an' our friend*

*   *   *   *   *   *   *

You're the poet of the people, where the red-mapped lands extend,
You're the poet of the jungle an' the lair, an' compare,
To the ever-speaking voice of everywhere."

M. F. MANSFIELD & COMPANY, NEW YORK

SUNG BY
MADAME CLARA BUTT.

No 1 in A♭.   No 2 in B♭.   No 3 in C

HAVE YOU NEWS OF MY BOY JACK?

SONG.

WORDS BY

RUDYARD KIPLING.

MUSIC BY

EDWARD GERMAN.

COPYRIGHT 1917.
ALL RIGHTS RESERVED.  PRICE 2/- NET.

THE WORDS OF THIS SONG ARE REPRINTED FROM MR. KIPLING'S "SEA WARFARE,"
BY PERMISSION OF THE AUTHOR.

Published by the
GENERAL PUBLISHING SOCIETY.
44, Berners Street, London, W.

KIPLING AND MUSIC

(1893–1971)

Kipling's first London lodgings, on the Embankment, were near Gatti's Music-Hall, where he was an enthusiastic patron. His rhythmic verses and emphatic refrains (like "pay—pay—pay!" in "The Absent-Minded Beggar," echoed by the audiences at its fund-raising recitals) reflected his love of popular music. Composers repaid the compliment, setting several of the Departmental Ditties, Barrack-Room Ballads, and many other poems to music. Among them were such distinguished artists as Sir Arthur Sullivan ("The Absent-Minded Beggar," shown in its musical edition elsewhere in this exhibition) and Sir Edward German. Other musicians such as Sir Edward Elgar and the American Randall Thompson were inspired to create symphonic pieces and operas based on Kipling works.

Musical Settings
of
Rudyard Kipling's
BARRACK ROOM BALLADS

The words of these songs are reprinted from Mr. Rudyard Kiplings' Barrack Room Ballads and Other Verses" by kind permission of Messrs Methuen & Co., London. Eng.

Copyright for All Countries

MANDALAY WALTZES   BEWICKE BEVERLEY. .75

White-Smith Music Pub. Co.
BOSTON   NEW YORK.   CHICAGO.

JOHN F. ELLIS & CO.,
937 PENNA. AVE.   WASHINGTON, D. C.

DANNY DEEVER.

WORDS BY.
RUDYARD KIPLING

MUSIC BY
GERARD F. COBB.

Moderato. ♩ = 92.

1. "What are the bu-gles blow-in' for? said Files-on-Pa-rade. "To turn you out, to turn you out," the
2. "What makes the rear-rank breathe so 'ard," said Files-on-Pa-rade. "Its bit-ter cold, its bit-ter cold," the
3. "Is cot was right-'and cot to mine," said Files-on-Pa-rade. "E's sleep-in' out an' far to night," the

Co-lour - Ser-geant said _____ "What makes you look so white, so white?" said
Co-lour - Ser-geant said _____ "What makes that front-rank man fall down?" says
Co-lour - Ser-geant said _____ "I've drunk 'is beer a score o' times," said

9710 = 4

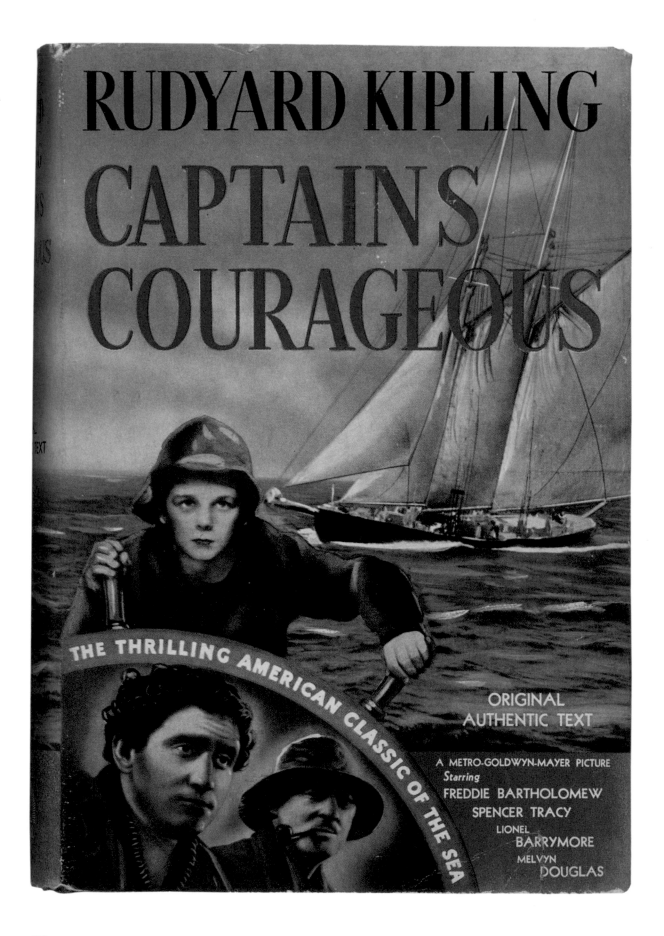

RUDYARD KIPLING
CAPTAINS COURAGEOUS

THE THRILLING AMERICAN CLASSIC OF THE SEA

ORIGINAL
AUTHENTIC TEXT

A METRO-GOLDWYN-MAYER PICTURE
Starring
FREDDIE BARTHOLOMEW
SPENCER TRACY
LIONEL BARRYMORE
MELVYN DOUGLAS

KIPLING ON STAGE AND SCREEN

(1903–2000)

Nothing Kipling wrote for the stage was published during his lifetime: *The Harbour Watch,* a one-act play produced at London's Royalty Theatre in 1913, was not published until 1990; *Upstairs* was found in his agent's files and printed in the *Times Literary Supplement* on 7 April 1995; and *The Jungle Play,* discovered in the author's papers at Sussex University, was published in April 2000. Adaptations by others, for both stage and screen, have been frequent. Thirty films have been made of Kipling's work to date (some of them much changed from his original stories and poems), almost evenly divided between silent (fourteen) and sound (sixteen); Kipling is known to have worked on some of those earlier scripts.

FRAMED ITEMS ON DISPLAY IN THE EXHIBITION

KIPLING BOOK AND MAGAZINE ADVERTISING POSTERS

The October Century. (New York: September 1891).

Kipling and His Work. by Fletcher C. Ransom (New York: October 1896).

The Seven Seas. (D. Appleton & Co., New York: 1896).
[Ill. p. 136]

"Captains Courageous". (The Century Co., New York: 1897).
[Ill. p. 137]

The Jungle Book. (The Century Co., New York: 1894).
[Ill. p. 138]

The Second Jungle Book. (The Century Co., New York: 1895).
[Ill. p. 139]

The Philistine. (East Aurora, NY: 1897). The magazine of Elbert Hubbard, publisher of the pirated edition of *The Dipsy Chanty.*

The Destroyers. (New York: April 1898). The American copyright edition of the poem was pulled, in four copies, from the types of the magazine.

KIPLING PORTRAITS

Rudyard Kipling *Soldiers Three* by "Spy" (Leslie Ward) Portrait, *Vanity Fair* Men of the Day No. 589, 7 June 1894
[Ill. p. 142–143]

Rudyard Kipling by R. Bryden. Woodcut from Bryden's *Woodcuts of Eminent Men of Letters of the Century* (November 1900).

Rudyard Kipling by William Nicholson. *Twelve Portraits* (first series), William Heinemann, London, September 1899.

Rudyard Kipling by William Strang, ARA. Final state of three, from an edition of about 80, of which it is thought about 60 were signed.
[Ill. p. 134]

Rudyard Kipling by Philip Burne-Jones. Monotone on Japanese vellum. Published 13 April 1900.

"Mr. Rudyard Kipling takes a bloomin' day aht, on the blasted heath, With Britannia, 'is gurl." by Max Beerbohm, from *The Poets' Corner* (Plate 24) (London: 1904).

Rudyard Kipling by James Ferguson. Original gouache prepared for *The Financial Times*, 22–23 January 1994.

New York Times Illustrated Magazine Supplement, March 5, 1899

Colliers Magazine, March 14, 1908, "Letters to the Family – I – The Eldest Sister"

Sunday Magazine of The New-York Tribune, April 28, 1907, "The Sons of Martha"

THE ABSENT-MINDED BEGGAR

The Absent-Minded Beggar. [*The Daily Mail* Color Illustrated Edition] (London: 1899). Damask cotton mat.

The Absent-Minded Beggar. [*The Daily Mail* Handkerchief Music Edition] (London: 1899). With portraits of British commander in chief Lord Frederick Roberts and Queen Victoria.
[Ill. p. 140]

The Absent-Minded Beggar. [First South African Edition] (Cape Town: 1900). Signed by Kipling, the first copy purchased at a Cape Town charity auction on 2 March 1900; one of two known copies.
[Ill. p. 141]

The Absent-Minded Beggar. [Announcement of] An Exhibition of the Works of Rudyard Kipling The Grolier Club of New York 1929 Copied From a Publication of *The Daily Mail*, 1899 Reissued Privately for Members of the Grolier Club, 1929.

A New Book
BY RUDYARD KIPLING

THE JUNGLE BOOK

Published by THE CENTURY Co.

For Sale Here ··· Price $1.50

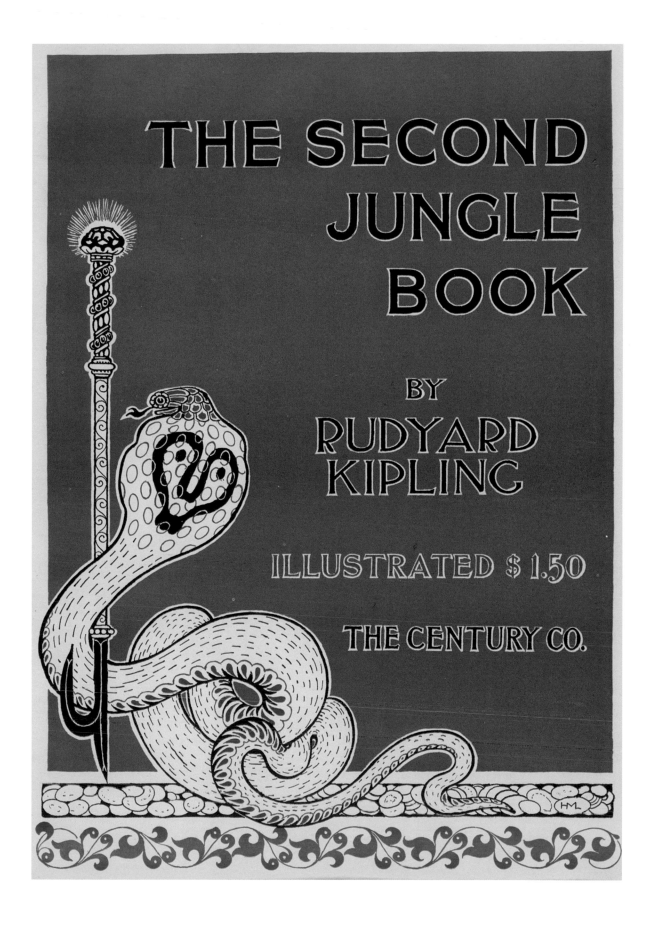

THE SECOND
JUNGLE
BOOK

BY
RUDYARD
KIPLING

ILLUSTRATED $ 1.50

THE CENTURY CO.

Lessee ... ... FRANK DE JONG.

Mr. Frank de Jong's and Herbert Flemming's New Company.

The Absent-Minded Beggar.

Recited by MISS MENA LE BERT

IN AID OF THE

"DAILY MAIL" RELIEF FUND.

WHEN you've shouted "Rule Britannia"—when
    you've sung "God Save the Queen"—
When you've finished killing Kruger with your
    mouth—
Will you kindly drop a shilling in my little tambourine
    For a gentleman in kharki ordered South?
He's an absent-minded beggar and his weaknesses are
    great—
    But we and Paul must take him as we find him—
He is out on active service, wiping something off a slate—
    And he's left a lot of little things behind him!

      Duke's son—cook's son—son of a hundred
        kings—
        (Fifty thousand horse and foot going to
        Table Bay!)
      Each of 'em doing his country's work (and
        who's to look after their things?)
        Pass the hat for your credit's sake, and pay—
        pay—pay!

There are girls he married secret, asking no permission to,
    For he knew he wouldn't get it if he did,
There is gas and coal and vittles, and the house-rent
    falling due,
    And it's more than rather likely there's a kid.
There are girls he walked with casual, they'll be sorry
    now he's gone,
    For an absent-minded beggar they will find him,
But it ain't the time for sermons with the winter coming
    on—
    We must help the girl that Tommy's left behind him!

      Cook's son—Duke's son—son of a belted Earl—
        Son of a Lambeth publican—it's all the same
        to-day!
      Each of 'em doing his country's work (and
        who's to look after the girl?)
        Pass the hat for your credit's sake, and pay—
        pay—pay!

There are families by thousands, far too proud to beg or
    speak—
    And they'll put their sticks and bedding up the spout,
And they'll live on half o' nothing paid 'em punctual
    once a week,
    'Cause the men that earned the wage is ordered out.
He's an absent-minded beggar, but he heard his country
    call,
    And his reg'ment didn't need to send to find him:
He chucked his job and joined it—so the job before us
    all
    Is to help the home that Tommy's left behind him!

      Duke's job—cook's job—gardener, baronet,
        groom—
        Mews or palace or paper-shop—there's some
        one gone away!
      Each of 'em doing his country's work (and
        who's to look after the room?—
        Pass the hat for your credit's sake, and pay—
        pay—pay!

Let us manage so as later we can look him in the face,
    And tell him—what he'd very much prefer—
That, while he saved the Empire, his employer saved
    his place,
    And his mates (that's you and me) looked out for her.
He's an absent-minded beggar, and he may forget it all,
    But we do not want his kiddies to remind him
That we sent 'em to the workhouse while their daddy
    hammered Paul,
So we'll help the homes our Tommy's left behind him!

      Cook's home—Duke's home—home of a
        millionaire.
        (Fifty thousand horse and foot going to Table
        Bay!)
      Each of 'em doing his country's work (and what
        have you got to spare?)
        Pass your hat for your credit's sake, and pay—
        pay—pay!

Rudyard Kipling

CAPE TIMES LIMITED.

Vincent Brooks, Day & Son, Lith.

"Soldiers Three"

MEN OF THE DAY. No. 589.

MR. RUDYARD KIPLING.

FOR all that he has done, for all the worth of his work, and for all the name that he has made, he is still quite young; having been born in Bombay scarce thirty years ago. He is also quite full of youth, which India has not been able to tame. His father, John Lockwood Kipling (who was Head Master of the Lahore School of Art), sent him home to Westward Ho, in Devonshire; where he learned what the United Services College could teach him. Like all boys he felt inclined to write, but unlike most boys he had the capacity as well as the inclination; and at the age of eighteen he went back to India to sub-edit *The Civil and Military Gazette* of Lahore. Presently his excellent handwriting, combined with his better style, made him dear to his employers; and he sent work to his own paper and to *The Pioneer* (of Allahabad) from the frontier at Rajputana and elsewhere that made him known as a very special correspondent. Then he published "Departmental Ditties" and "Plain Tales from the Hills"; which were presently followed by half-a-dozen little books of military, native, and social life in India. And very soon the excellence of his work became known in England; where he quickly earned a literary reputation that amazed the critics, yet has steadily grown ever since. Five years ago he left India to see China, Japan, and America; after which he came to London and got married. He has now made himself an American home in Vermont; and when he has passed seven years in the study of the people among whom he dwells, we may expect to have a great work on that country which has in it the making of several Empires.

From the time when he first began to write tales for the Indian Press he has shown a quick power of vivid description that is quite unique; and as he writes only of what he knows, his stories of Anglo-Indian life, especially as to the military side of it, are remarkable for their striking fidelity. His "Soldiers Three" would alone have made a great man's reputation; and though he has been guilty of less good work yet has he not been spoiled by success. For he has in him neither the making of a pot-boiler nor the grub of the literary hack. Much that he has written in prose is incomparable with any living man's work; while his "Barrack-Room Ballads" and other verses show that he is possessed of a Muse of brilliant style, rhythmical power, and complete originality. His fault, if he have one, is that he thinks too highly of other people's wits; so that his stories are often like too strong food undiluted. Yet it may be said that to those stout minds which are able to prefer condensed extract of meat to English beef, this is no fault, but the reverse. With all his success he is a good, unaffected fellow, who can keep a roomful of intelligent people listening to the charm of his easy talk with profit and pleasure; for he is a man exceedingly well-informed on unknown matters, who has a great knack of imparting ready knowledge on most subjects without seeming to teach. He is an artist who has created a style for himself. He is also a nephew of Sir Edward Burne-Jones.

He was not popular with all the ladies of India; but he proposes some day to build for himself a small cottage in England.